The Peach Tree Tea Room
Cookbook

by

CYNTHIA COLLINS PEDREGON

THE PEACH TREE GIFT GALLERY and TEA ROOM

FREDERICKSBURG, TEXAS

Cover Design & Illustrations

by Becky Crouch Patterson

Photographs

by Marc Bennett
White Oak Studio

Calligraphy

by Enid Collins

Copyright © 1990
by
Peach Tree Gift Gallery & Tea Room
210 South Adams Street
Fredericksburg, Texas 78624
(512) 997-9527

ISBN 0-9627590-7-4
Library of Congress Catalog Card # 90-062706

Printed in the USA by
WIMMER BROTHERS
A Wimmer Company
Memphis • Dallas

Dedication

To David, Tina, and Carlos — for them and theirs — may the tradition continue!

To Hector, and a lifetime of adventures — past, present and future — together!

With gratitude to God who faithfully leads me and is constantly showing and teaching me that "all things work together for good to those who love Him and are called according to His purpose."

Romans 8:28.

History of the Peach Tree

When Cynthia and I sit and reflect about The Peach Tree, we realize how fleeting time has been since the spring of 1972, when we began the restoration work on our building. We acquired the building quite by chance. At the time I was manager of Collins of Texas, a family-owned handbag manufacturing business. Needing additional warehouse space, I inquired with a local realtor about potential property. Knowing of my interest in historic restoration, he mentioned the property on Adams Street — a beautiful German limestone residence which he thought we would enjoy seeing. Little did I know that what started as the pursuit of additional warehouse space would turn into a change in my career. Although I informed him we were in our "nesting period," a young family with two toddlers and hardly able to afford restoring the building, he insisted on giving me the keys to the house in case we had an opportunity to see it over the weekend.

After church on Sunday the house keys dropped out of my pocket on the way to our car, which reminded me to go by and see the place. Cynthia's mother was with us that day as we stopped by the house to inspect it. While walking through the house the three of us talked about the potential uses for the property. Three hours later we agreed this house really would make a wonderful store location! Driving home that afternoon, we felt in our hearts we had to have it. If we were to purchase this house, we would open our own gift store.

I called the realtor to tell him we were definitely interested in the house and asked if we could talk about it on Monday. He suggested we meet at his office that same afternoon and continue our conversation. We did, and before the day was over, it was "a done deal" as we say in Texas. The very next day I went to the office to give notice of my resignation. In a matter of hours that Sunday afternoon the decision to start our own family business was made. We opened The Peach Tree on July 13, 1972. I must say, we have really enjoyed this business. It has truly been a blessing to our family.

In the fall of 1984, we opened the Tea Room and this new venture began another wonderful chapter in the life of the Pedregon family. We opened with five tables, and we never envisioned serving any more than coffee, teas and desserts. Cynthia not only prepared all the desserts, she was also our only waitress. She had one helper in the kitchen. On weekends our son David, 16 years old at the time, would help wait on tables; our 12 year old, Carlos, would help wash dishes; and Tina and I would work in the gift shop.

Our customers were very supportive and encouraging. We ended a very successful Christmas season that year and after the holidays, at the encouragement of customers and friends, Cynthia began serving lunches on Fridays and Saturdays. Cynthia's reputation as a fine cook was greeted with sincere compliments from our customers — and she received it like applause to an actress on stage. In the months following, more space was devoted to food service, more staff people came on board, and we increased our serving days to six, Monday through Saturday. Our sideline had now become a separate business! Our shop and Tea Room now employ 25 people on staff.

As a result of Cynthia's wonderful creativity, we now present this collection of recipes. May you enjoy her book, and may we have the pleasure of your company in our shop and Tea Room soon!

Most cordially,

Hector Pedregon

With a Grateful Heart.....

To Carol Bade and Judy Morgan for the long hours and late nights of typing, proofing, and editing — especially their great care and concern for detail and accuracy.

To Lydia, Evelyn, Vicky, and Maria, who have worked by my side since we started this cookbook — for their encouragement and help.

To all those here at work who delayed dieting until the recipe testing and tasting was completed!

To David, Tina, and Carlos, who bounce back every time the business preempts their time.

To Hector, the love of my life, companion, partner, and my best friend — my love and gratitude.

To my Mother — for my earliest cooking lessons and the loving affirmation she's given me these many years.

To my Dad — with whom this would have been such fun to share.

A Note from Cynthia

It's an awesome, truly awesome task — this business of writing a cookbook — especially one that is so incredibly personal, resulting from a lifetime of memories. I am forced to slow down and recall family customs, traditions, experiences — all in great detail, rather like taking time to write a long letter!

Ever since I was a little girl I've loved to cook. My parents were both fine artists. I grew up surrounded by good taste — in fact, my mother was often quick to point out to me what was "tacky" or unacceptable in artwork or clothing. The first art lessons I remember were those in the family kitchen preparing for Thanksgiving dinner. My brother, Jeep, and I would polish all the silver for the table. Then my project was to arrange the relish trays attractively. My mother would tell me, "Part of the appeal, Cynth, is how food is presented — it must look pretty so as to spark one's interest in the first place." I took that lesson to heart and would go to great pains to arrange foods. Years later, as I would spend days getting ready for parties, she would remark, "Really, Cynth, that's a lot of trouble for something that people are only going to eat!" But the impression had been made early in my life — indelibly!

I owe much of my love for cooking to my mother, Mim, because when I was very young she turned the kitchen over to me. We lived on a small ranch in the Texas Hill Country 14 miles from Medina, where the family business was located. When we got home in the evenings I'd head for the kitchen, and she to care for the flowers in her garden. It was a wonderful time for me — I had free rein in the kitchen and was allowed to create whatever I wanted. Much of my self-esteem developed from the cultivation of this talent — I believe that everyone must be encouraged to grow and blossom in the gift God gives them. I treasure the encouragement I received from my family!

One of the greatest influences on my career was my Aunt Jo. She was the originator of Hamburg Heaven in New York City in the early 1930's, during the Depression Years. When everyone else was charging 5 cents for hamburgers, she embellished hers like gourmet feasts and charged 25 cents! She made elegant hamburgers and her restaurant was very popular with the elite, after-theatre crowd.

From the time I was little I was impressed with her ability to take the simplest ingredients and turn them into something wonderful. We'd look into the fridge together and I'd see nothing, but she would put together a feast — so creative she was! I was always excited when she visited. It meant we could cook together — and I loved that! Many of the recipes we use today in the Tea Room are an outgrowth of those wonderful cooking times we spent together. Cooking was natural for her — not fussy food, not trendy or faddish, but sensible food. She'd tell me to "cook sensibly" — to be sure, I didn't get any "frilly" influences from my Aunt Jo!

I was also influenced by Roberta Stieler Warren. She and my mother had attended college together, and when I moved to Fredericksburg as a young bride, she included me in many activities and made me feel welcome right away. I was immediately inspired by her style of entertaining — she has a remarkable knack of drawing from her Texas and German heritage when hostessing an elegant event, whether serving in her spacious ranch house or her tiny restored log cabin. Just by observing her gracious gift for entertaining, I was encouraged to treasure my own roots. The Texas Hill Country has a rich heritage and I feel warm gratitude to Roberta and others like her, who have kept valuable traditions going by inspiring us "younger" women.

When we moved to Fredericksburg, it was just beginning its growth — young families were returning because of the wholesome environment and strong emphasis on traditional family values. We formed some really special friendships with some other young couples. A supper club grew out of these friendships. We met once a month faithfully for many years. As for exotic cuisine — you name it, we tried it! We had some wonderfully extravagant evenings. On one occasion we prepared dinner around a Greek theme — and when sharing recipes afterwards, we realized we had consumed about a quart of olive oil among the eight of us!

It was out of this supper club that my cooking relationship with Carol Bade developed. Little did any of us imagine that years later we would add a tea room and catering business to The Peach Tree and that Carol would become our Manager. We both share a strong love for entertaining — Carol likes the planning and decorating and this gives me the freedom to do what I enjoy the most — preparing the food. Our caterings have become "events" with Carol's beautiful floral arrangements enhancing the food we prepare. It's been a special working arrangement and we've both grown immensely through these experiences, both professionally and in our personal lives.

I believe one of the greatest gifts we can receive is to be able to enjoy being at work and doing what we love, all at the same time. I have been blessed with this gift — cooking to me is pure joy — the kitchen is the place where nurturing takes place. When the children were little, it was important that we have a kitchen table where we could share together as a family at any time during the day.

The Tea Room kitchen has been an extension of this for me. Our little Peach Tree family begins early each morning with 3 of us in the kitchen — growing to 12 to 15 by noontime. Sometimes we are like stones in the tumbling machine with our rough edges being rubbed off — but mostly its been the most affirming place I've ever entered. Sometimes when people see me in the dining room they ask, "Do you do all this cooking?", I'm reminded of the words from the song "I get by with a little help from my friends!"

The Tea Room has come a long, long way since those early days when I did the work all by myself. There have been some rough spots, but mainly we have had good times. I am truly a blessed person. May you be greatly blessed and receive joy in preparing these recipes. I present them to you with love! *Love, Cynthia* ♡

the Peach Tree Tea Room and Gift Gallery by John Austin Hanna

Table of Contents

party Grazing
foods
Appetizers
and
Snacks

Fresh Herb Dip

8 ounces cream cheese, room temperature
2 cloves garlic, minced
¼ cup chopped fresh parsley
¼ cup chopped green onion (mostly green part)
½ cup sour cream
2 to 4 tablespoons light cream or milk, optional
Salt and pepper to taste

1. Using an electric mixer or food processor, blend softened cream cheese. Add garlic, parsley, and green onion. Mix well.
2. Add sour cream, thoroughly mixing and scraping sides of bowl. Thin if necessary with light cream or milk. Taste for salt and pepper. Refrigerate. Best if made the day before.

Makes 1¾ cups.

Oyster - Spinach Dip

A really great dip for parties — always a favorite with men!

1 medium onion, finely chopped
2 tablespoons butter
1 10-ounce package frozen, chopped spinach, thawed and squeezed dry
2 2¾-ounce cans smoked oysters, drained and finely chopped
2 cups sour cream
2 tablespoons lemon juice
1 tablespoon Worcestershire sauce
½ teaspoon Tabasco
½ cup mayonnaise
Salt and pepper to taste

1. Sauté onion in butter. Allow to cool.
2. Add remaining ingredients and mix well. Refrigerate several hours or overnight. It will thicken as it chills. Serve with crackers.

Makes 4 cups.

Herb Butter

This is a popular addition to our catered events. We serve it in a wooden heart bowl, garnished with a sprig of rosemary or oregano and a bright yellow cosmos bloom!

1 pound butter, softened
1 to 2 teaspoons coarse, ground black pepper
1 clove garlic, minced
½ cup finely chopped fresh herbs (try a combination of dill, oregano, lemon balm, salad burnet, thyme)

1. Using a food processor or electric mixer, cream butter until smooth and creamy.
2. Add remaining ingredients and process just until mixed.
3. Mold into desired shape and chill.

Hill Country Pecan Spread

If you are lucky enough to have this spread left over, it is terrific warmed and served as a topping for baked potatoes. Great served warm with wheat crackers.

1 8-ounce package cream cheese, softened
2 tablespoons milk
2 ounces dried beef, chopped
¼ cup chopped green pepper
2 tablespoons minced onion
½ cup sour cream
½ teaspoon minced garlic
¼ teaspoon pepper
1 to 2 tablespoons chopped pickled jalapeños
2 tablespoons butter
½ cup chopped pecans

1. Using an electric mixer, blend together softened cream cheese and milk. Stir in dried beef, green pepper, onion, sour cream, garlic, pepper, and jalapeños. Mix well. Pour into 1 quart baking dish.
2. Melt butter in small skillet, add pecans and sauté over medium heat until light brown. Spread over cream cheese mixture, and bake in a pre-heated 350 degree oven for 20 minutes.

Serves 8 - 10.

Surprise Spinach Spread

This dip has been popular at all our catered parties. It is best when made the day before serving.

    1 10-ounce package frozen chopped spinach, thawed
    1 cup mayonnaise
    1 cup sour cream
    1 1.4-ounce package Knorr vegetable soup mix. (This mix
      cannot be substituted.)
    1 8½-ounce can water chestnuts, drained and finely chopped
    ¼ cup finely chopped onion
    ½ cup grated carrots
    ½ cup chopped red pepper

1. Squeeze all water from spinach. Combine with other ingredients and refrigerate for at least 2 hours. Serve with crackers, raw carrot sticks, or jicama sticks.

Serves 12.

Curry Almond Spread

We have served this on our sandwich buffets. It's delicious spread on raisin pumpernickel bread and topped with peppered ham or smoked turkey.

    16 ounces cream cheese, room temperature
    ½ teaspoon dry mustard
    2 teaspoons curry powder
    ½ cup chopped Major Grey's chutney
    ½ cup toasted and slivered almonds

1. Using an electric mixer, blend cream cheese with dry mustard and curry powder. Add chutney and mix well.
2. Form into ball and chill. Roll in toasted and slivered almonds.

Makes 2 cups.

Cream Cheese, Olive and Walnut Spread

As a teenager, one of my favorite after-school snacks was a cream cheese and olive sandwich. The addition of black olives and walnuts makes this more wonderful as a sandwich filling, or as a spread for crackers.

12 ounces cream cheese, room temperature
¾ cup roasted and chopped walnuts
¼ cup chopped or sliced stuffed green olives
½ cup chopped or sliced pitted black olives

1. Using an electric mixer, beat cream cheese until creamy. Stir in remaining ingredients.

Makes 3 cups.

Jalapeño-Pimento Cheese Spread

This is such a basic spread that I almost did not include it here. But it's so delicious, I didn't want to overlook it. It's especially good on raisin pumpernickel bread. It would also be terrific on a sandwich made with bacon, lettuce and tomato.

3 cups grated Cheddar cheese
1½ cups grated Monterey Jack cheese
½ cup chopped pimentos
2 tablespoons chopped pickled jalapeños with juice
1 cup good quality mayonnaise
1 cup Miracle Whip

1. Combine all ingredients and mix well.

Makes 6 cups.

Jezebel Sweet Hot Sauce

This is the sauce that we serve at all our catered events. It is delicious with all meats, and keeps forever in the refrigerator.

1 18-ounce jar pineapple preserves
1 18-ounce jar apple jelly
¼ cup dry mustard
1 5-ounce jar horseradish

1. In saucepan, combine pineapple preserves and apple jelly. Heat, stirring with a whisk until melted and thoroughly mixed.
2. Gradually add mustard, blending well.
3. Remove from heat and add horseradish. Mix well. Refrigerate.

Makes 4 cups.

Hidden Valley Cheese Ball

This is a good recipe for the holidays. We mixed a large amount and formed a Christmas tree for one of our catered parties - chopped parsley for leaves, pimento garlands, and black olives. It was a delicious and dramatic presentation.

16 ounces cream cheese, room temperature
.4 ounce package Hidden Valley Original Ranch salad dressing mix (buttermilk recipe)
2 cups grated Cheddar cheese
Garnish: Chopped parsley or chopped nuts

1. Using an electric mixer or food processor, blend cream cheese and Hidden Valley mix.
2. Add Cheddar cheese and mix well.
3. Form into ball or place in crock. May be covered with chopped parsley or finely chopped nuts.

Makes 3½ cups.

Goat Cheese Cheesecake

This was prepared for the first time at the opening of our G. Harvey Gallery. I wanted to have Texas Hill Country products represented for this grand occasion. Garnished with sun-dried tomatoes and fresh basil, it made a nice Texas statement.

Crust:
    1½ cups fresh breadcrumbs
    ½ cup melted butter
    3 tablespoons grated Romano cheese
    1 clove garlic, minced

1. Combine all crust ingredients and pat the mixture into bottom of 10" springform pan. Refrigerate.

Filling:
    28 ounces cream cheese, room temperature
    4 eggs
    ⅓ cup half and half, or evaporated milk
    1 cup sour cream
    ½ teaspoon salt
    1 cup goat cheese
    ¼ cup sun-dried tomatoes, coarsely chopped, optional
    2 tablespoons fresh herbs (such as basil, thyme, and/or
        oregano)
    1 clove garlic, minced

1. Using a food processor, or electric mixer, blend cream cheese. Add eggs, one at a time, beating well after each addition.
2. Add remaining ingredients and mix well. Pour mixture into chilled crust.
3. Place springform pan on cookie sheet and bake in a pre-heated 325 degree oven for 1 hour. Turn off oven and let cool with door closed for 30 minutes. Remove from oven, cool completely, and refrigerate.

Serves 30 as an appetizer.

Bleu Cheese Mousse

This is a lovely, light tasting spread. Try it served with crackers or pear and apple slices. It is especially nice to unmold on a ring of grape leaves with grape clusters nearby.

1 egg, separated
½ cup whipping cream
8 ounces bleu cheese, room temperature
4 ounces cream cheese, room temperature
¼ cup butter, room temperature
1 tablespoon unflavored gelatin
¼ cup cold water
½ teaspoon Dijon mustard

1. Beat egg white until stiff and set aside.
2. In another bowl, whip cream until stiff and set aside.
3. Using an electric mixer, beat egg yolk. Add bleu cheese, cream cheese, and butter, beating until smooth.
4. Stir gelatin into cold water. Then place dish of gelatin in hot water and stir until dissolved. Add gelatin and mustard to cheese mixture.
5. Fold in egg white and then fold in whipped cream. Pour into oiled 1 quart mold. Chill until firm. Unmold onto platter.

Note: When serving apple or pear slices on a buffet, dip them first in pineapple juice so they will not darken!

Shrimp Mold

For catered buffets, we mold this in a fish mold and decorate it with thinly sliced cucumbers for scales and an olive for the eye. Circle it with fresh dill and pretty sea shells for a dramatic effect.

1 10-ounce can condensed tomato soup
8 ounces cream cheese, softened
2 tablespoons unflavored gelatin
½ cup cold water
1 cup mayonnaise
16 ounces frozen cooked shrimp, thawed and chopped (a food
   processor is great for this)
1 small onion, finely chopped
½ cup finely chopped celery
2 teaspoons lemon juice
¼ cup capers
1 teaspoon paprika
Salt, pepper and garlic salt to taste

1. Heat soup and carefully mix in softened cream cheese. Stir well to completely blend.

2. Dissolve gelatin in cold water and add to hot soup mixture, mixing well. Cool for 30 minutes.

3. Add mayonnaise, blending well. Add remaining ingredients. Pour mixture into oiled mold.

4. Refrigerate overnight. Unmold on lettuce-lined platter. Serve with crackers.

Serves 30 as a spread.

Mushroom Paté

This is a very rich appetizer - elegant if you serve it in a sparkling crystal bowl garnished with fresh herbs. Can be served either chilled or at room temperature.

2 green onions, minced
1 pound mushrooms, finely chopped (a food processor is great for this)
½ cup softened butter, divided
6 ounces cream cheese, room temperature
1 teaspoon lemon juice
½ cup chopped walnuts
1 teaspoon Tabasco
Salt to taste
Garnish: Sour cream and chopped fresh parsley

1. Sauté the green onions and chopped mushrooms in ¼ cup butter. Cook over low heat for 30 minutes, or until all the liquid is absorbed.

2. Remove from heat. Add cream cheese and stir until melted. Add lemon juice, walnuts, Tabasco, and the remaining ¼ cup butter. Add salt to taste.

3. Transfer the mixture to a glass bowl, and chill. Before serving spread the top with sour cream and decorate with fresh parsley.

Serves 10 - 12.

Chicken Liver Paté

Peggy Cox, who is on our staff, prepared this dish the first time we catered together and it got raves! Men love this dish, even those who hesitate to eat liver. Serve it with our German beer rye and Pommery mustard.

1 medium onion, coarsely chopped
1 clove garlic, minced
2 eggs
1 pound raw chicken livers
¼ cup flour
¼ cup butter, softened
1 cup heavy cream
½ teaspoon ginger
½ teaspoon allspice
1 teaspoon salt
1 teaspoon white pepper
Garnish: Whipped cream cheese

1. This recipe must be made in a blender, not a food processor. Combine onion, garlic, and eggs in blender. Blend at high speed for 1 minute.

2. Add chicken livers and blend 2 more minutes on high speed.

3. Add remaining ingredients, blending on high for 2 minutes until smooth.

4. Pour into well-greased 1 quart baking dish. Cover with foil and set dish in pan of hot water. Bake in a pre-heated 325 degree oven for 3 hours.

5. Remove foil and cool. Cover with plastic wrap and chill overnight. This may be unmolded if desired. It may be garnished with softened whipped cream cheese, piped in a decorative border around edges. Serve with crackers, Cynthia's Famous French Bread, or pumpernickel.

Serves 24.

Black Bean Paté
with Green Onion Sauce

4 cups dried black beans, sorted and rinsed
1 large onion, chopped
3" piece of ginger, peeled and chopped, optional
6 cloves garlic, minced
3 tablespoons butter or oil
1 cup sour cream
6 eggs
2 teaspoons salt
1 tablespoon pepper

1. Cover rinsed beans with water. Bring to boil. Cook beans in rapidly boiling water for about 1 hour until beans are soft. When done, drain beans in colander until cool and dry as possible.

2. Sauté onion, garlic, and optional ginger in the butter or oil until soft and transparent. Set aside.

3. Coarsely chop black beans in food processor. In large bowl, combine beans with onion mixture, sour cream, eggs, salt and pepper. Mix well.

4. Place paté in a buttered loaf pan or tureen. Cover with buttered foil and place pan into larger baking dish filled halfway with hot water. Bake in a pre-heated 350 degree oven for 1 hour and 20 minutes or until firm. Cool completely, slice, and serve with green onion sauce.

Serves 16 - 18.

Green Onion Sauce:
1 egg yolk
½ cup red wine vinegar
2 tablespoons Dijon mustard
4 green onions
3 cloves garlic
1 teaspoon sugar
1½ cups olive oil
Salt, pepper to taste

1. Combine first 6 ingredients in bowl of food processor. Process until well blended.

2. While machine is running, add olive oil in slow, steady stream. Taste for salt and pepper.

Crisp Vegetable Marinade

This looks pretty in a lettuce lined bowl, garnished with whole cherry tomatoes, and it's great for calorie counters at summer buffets.

1½ cups cider vinegar
1 cup salad oil
¼ cup sugar
1 teaspoon oregano
1 teaspoon parsley flakes
¼ teaspoon pepper
2 teaspoons salt
½ cup water
1 small cauliflower, cut into flowerets
2 pounds carrots, pared and cut into thin diagonal slices
8 celery ribs, cut into 1" slices
2 green peppers, cut into strips
8 ounces pimento, drained and cut into strips, or fresh red
  pepper strips
1 6-ounce jar stuffed green olives, drained
1 cup whole pitted black olives, drained
2 14-ounce cans artichoke hearts, drained and cut in half
1 15-ounce can baby corn on the cob, drained

1. Combine vinegar, oil, sugar, oregano, parsley, pepper, salt and water in large sauce pan. Bring to boil.

2. Place remaining ingredients in large bowl. Pour hot liquid over, and toss lightly.

3. Cover, and refrigerate for at least 24 hours. Toss occasionally. Drain before serving.

Serves 35 as an appetizer.

Marinated Carrot Sticks

I always enjoy having these on hand - they make great party munchies!

8 carrots, peeled and cut into 3" sticks
3 tablespoons apple cider vinegar
3 tablespoons oil
1 clove garlic, minced
1 teaspoon Jane's Krazy Mixed-Up Salt
½ teaspoon sugar
Chopped parsley

1. Combine all ingredients except the parsley. Marinate overnight. Drain and garnish with chopped parsley.

Serves 8 - 10.

Hot Apple Cider

This not only tastes delicious, it gives the whole house a festive aroma! I keep it on hand in the fridge during the holidays!

6 cinnamon sticks
1 teaspoon whole allspice
2 teaspoons whole cloves
¼ cup brown sugar or honey
1 gallon apple cider
1 quart cranberry juice
2 teaspoons Tang or orange peel

1. Place first 3 ingredients in a cheesecloth bag.
2. Combine spice bag with remaining ingredients in a large stock pot.
3. Bring to boil, reduce heat and simmer 20 minutes. Remove spice bag and serve warm.

Makes 20 cups.

Orange Cooler

1 16-ounce can frozen orange juice
2 cans water
1 liter gingerale or ½ liter gingerale and ½ liter club soda

1. Mix orange juice and water in punch bowl or large pitcher.
2. At the last minute, add gingerale and/or club soda. Add ice and more water if necessary.

Makes 13 6-ounce servings or 10 8-ounce servings.

Note: Champagne may be added for a mimosa punch.

New Year's Eve Wine Punch

This is the punch that we served for many years at our traditional New Year's Eve party. It's light and delicious - a good choice for parties and receptions. Sometimes I like to add 1 to 2 quarts of club soda for sparkle.

1 cup light simple syrup
2 cups orange juice
1 cup pineapple juice
¼ cup lemon juice
½ cup brandy
2 fifths chilled Sauterne
Strawberries
Citrus slices

1. Make simple syrup by combining ⅔ cup sugar and ⅔ cup water. Heat until sugar is dissolved. Allow to cool.
2. Combine the juices and simple syrup. Chill well.
3. Just before serving, add brandy, Sauterne and ice. Garnish with strawberries and citrus slices.

Makes 12 cups.

Notes

_____

_____

_____

_____

_____

_____

_____

_____

_____

_____

_____

_____

_____

Soup, Beautiful Soup

Chilled Creamy Cucumber Soup

3 medium cucumbers, peeled, seeded, and cut in chunks
3 cups Swanson's chicken broth, divided
1½ cups sour cream
1½ cups buttermilk or plain yogurt
3 tablespoons white vinegar
1 garlic clove, minced
½ cup sliced green onion
2 fresh tomatoes, peeled and chopped
½ cup chopped parsley
Salt to taste
Garnish: Toasted almond slices

1. Process cucumber chunks in blender or food processor a very short time with ½ cup chicken broth. Be careful not to overblend.

2. In a large bowl, combine all remaining ingredients except tomatoes, parsley, and almonds. Mix well and chill thoroughly.

3. Before serving, stir in tomatoes and parsley. Garnish with toasted almond slices.

Serves 6 - 8.

Health note: Substitute yogurt for the sour cream!

Peach Tree
Chilled Avocado Soup

If I had to name our single most popular soup in the Tea Room, this would be the one. Our customers love it! It is one of our regular daily soups during the summer months.

4 medium ripe avocados, peeled and pitted
1 garlic clove, minced
4 green onions, chopped
5 tablespoons chopped fresh cilantro
1 tablespoon sliced pickled jalapeños with juice
½ teaspoon Tabasco
3 cups sour cream
1 cup buttermilk
8 cups chilled Swanson's chicken broth
Salt to taste
Garnish: Sour cream and finely minced green onions (green part only)

1. In a blender or food processor, combine avocados, garlic, green onions, cilantro, jalapeños and juice, and Tabasco. Process until smooth. Add sour cream and process again.

2. Stir in buttermilk and chilled chicken broth. Taste for salt. Cover and refrigerate until very cold. Garnish with a dollop of sour cream and chopped green onions, green part only.

Serves 12 to 14.

Iced Pimento Soup

1 cup chopped onion
¼ cup butter
¼ cup flour
5 cups Swanson's chicken broth
2 4-ounce jars pimentos, drained
2 cups half and half
Salt and white pepper to taste

1. Sauté onion in butter until soft. Stir in flour and cook over low heat for 1 minute. Do not allow flour to burn.

2. Add chicken broth and cook, stirring constantly, until thickened. Remove from heat and allow to cool slightly.

3. Place in food processor or blender. Add pimentos and blend well.

4. Place mixture in large bowl. Add half and half, salt and pepper to taste, blending well. Chill thoroughly. Crème fraîche or thinned sour cream will be pretty swirled in. Add a dill sprig if you have it — it will make a pretty spring accent.

Serves 8.

Today
Texas Quiche
Soups
Jalapeno-Potato
Chilled Avocado
Desserts
Collins Chocolate
Cake
Peach Crepe

Welcome to the Peach Tree Tea Room !

Christmas Gifts made by local Fredericksburg
craftsmen and artists

Love one another that your joy may be full

Love Banner, designed by Enid Collins, and stitched by the Fountain Walk Artisans.

Trio: Veggie sandwich with chilled avocado soup ♥
Chicken mousse with mushroom paté ♥ Avocado
mousse with fresh fruit ♥

Gazpacho

This is Carol Bade's wonderful Gazpacho soup recipe from pre-Tea Room days. We both worked in the gift shop and we would bring our lunches to work. I would always want to trade with Carol for her Gazpacho. It's the best I've ever tasted! Before we adapted it to the Tea Room, it had olive oil and red wine vinegar. Perhaps it wasn't as slimming as this recipe, but it was worth splurging a little.

1 garlic clove
1 small yellow onion
5 large fresh tomatoes, peeled
2 small cucumbers, peeled and seeded
1 green pepper, seeded
1 46-ounce can tomato juice
2 tablespoons cider vinegar
½ teaspoon salt
1 teaspoon pepper
¼ teaspoon Tabasco
¼ cup chopped parsley
Garnish: Unpeeled cucumber slices and fresh dill

1. In a large food processor, chop garlic and onion and tomatoes. Remove from processor and place in a large bowl.

2. In the processor coarsely chop peeled and seeded cucumbers and seeded green pepper. It is important that they are not chopped too finely.

3. Add cucumbers and pepper to tomato mixture. Add remaining ingredients and adjust seasonings. May need to add additional tomato juice as it thickens. Chill thoroughly. This is best made the day before serving. Garnish with unpeeled cucumber slices and fresh dill.

Serves 12 to 14.

Celery Almondine Soup

The old original Gallery Restaurant in Fredericksburg used to serve sautéed celery. It was one of my favorite vegetable side dishes. Sue Bellows and I developed this recipe using the same ingredients — very light and elegant!

2 cups diced onions
½ cup butter or margarine
2 bunches of celery with leaves, sliced thinly
8 cups chicken broth
2 cups evaporated milk
¾ teaspoon white pepper
Salt to taste
Garnish: Toasted almond slices

1. In stock pot sauté onions in butter, or margarine, until soft. Add chopped celery and quickly sauté until celery is tender-crisp, about 5 minutes.

2. Add chicken broth and bring just to a boil. Don't overcook this soup; you want the celery to keep its pretty bright green color!

3. Add milk and pepper. Taste for salt. Heat and serve. Garnish with lightly toasted almond slices.

Serves 12 - 14.

Cauliflower Soup

Please try this one - you will love it! The rice does the thickening. Health note: If you substitute skim milk for the heavy cream, you can down this guilt free!

1½ pounds fresh cauliflower, leaves trimmed, core removed,
    and broken into flowerets
1 small carrot, peeled and sliced
6 cups chicken broth
⅓ cup uncooked long grain rice
2 cups milk (or 1 cup water and 1 cup evaporated milk)
1 tablespoon lemon juice
¼ teaspoon freshly grated nutmeg
¼ teaspoon cayenne pepper
½ cup heavy cream or evaporated milk
Salt to taste
Garnish: Chopped fresh chives or nutmeg

1. Place the cauliflower in a medium saucepan. Add the carrot and the chicken broth. Heat to boiling. Stir in the rice and reduce the heat. Simmer, uncovered, 30 minutes. Remove from heat.

2. Place half the cauliflower mixture into the container of a processor or blender with 1 cup of the milk. Process until smooth, being very careful, as hot liquid will expand.

3. Transfer the mixture to a medium saucepan. Repeat the process with the remaining cauliflower mixture and milk. Add this to the saucepan.

4. Add the lemon juice, nutmeg, cayenne pepper, ½ cup cream or evaporated milk, and salt to taste. Heat through. Garnish with chives or a sprinkling of grated nutmeg. (Soup may be served cold, thinned with milk after chilling.)

Serves 8.

Fresh Squash Soup

A tasty variation would be to add sliced green chiles, corn, and chicken too!

¼ pound lean bacon, diced
1 large onion, chopped
2 cloves garlic, minced
8 large yellow squash, sliced
2 large zucchini, sliced
8 cups chicken broth
5 teaspoons comino
1½ teaspoons oregano
4 cups evaporated milk
Salt and pepper to taste
Garnish: Grated Cheddar cheese, chopped green onion, and
   pimento strips

1. In a large stock pot brown diced bacon. Discard all but 2 tablespoons of bacon grease. Add onion and sauté until transparent Add garlic.

2. Add yellow squash, zucchini, chicken broth, comino and oregano. Bring to boil, reduce heat and simmer, covered, for about 10 minutes.

3. Add evaporated milk and heat through. Using a potato masher, coarsely mash squash. Taste for salt and pepper. Optional - half the soup may be puréed. Garnish with grated Cheddar cheese, chopped green onion, and pimento strips.

Serves 16.

Pumpkin Soup

Be sure to try this soup. When we offer our customers a taste of it in our Tea Room, we always serve every bit of it. You just have to try that first bite!

2 16-ounce cans pumpkin
¼ teaspoon allspice
½ teaspoon ground nutmeg
½ teaspoon cinnamon
10 cups chicken broth
2 tablespoons butter or margarine
1 cup chopped yellow onions
1 cup cleaned and sliced leeks
Salt and white pepper to taste
Garnish: Sour cream, nutmeg, and chives

1. In a large stock pot, combine pumpkin, allspice, nutmeg, cinnamon and broth. Bring to a boil, reduce heat and simmer, covered, for 30 minutes.

2. In a separate saucepan, melt the butter or margarine over medium heat. Sauté the onion and leeks until golden, about 6 to 8 minutes. Stir into the pumpkin mixture and heat for several minutes, stirring constantly. Taste for salt and white pepper. Serve very hot with a dollop of sour cream on top and a pinch of nutmeg and chopped green onion tops.

Note: This soup should be a little spicy. If the soup is too thick, thin it with additional broth.

Serves 12.

Zucchini and Brown Rice Soup

Try this soup when you are short on time, but still want something tasty. A delicious variation could be made by adding cooked, thinly sliced chicken. Add this one to your list when you have to count calories!

1 pound zucchini
½ pound fresh spinach or Swiss chard
8 cups chicken broth
½ cup uncooked brown rice
1½ cups sliced yellow onions
3 tablespoons butter or margarine
Salt and pepper to taste

1. Wash, trim, and grate the zucchini. Wash the spinach or chard, and cut into thin strips.

2. Bring the broth to a boil and stir in the rice. Reduce heat, and simmer, covered, until the rice is just tender - about 40 minutes.

3. In a large pan, sauté onions in the butter or margarine until wilted and golden. Add zucchini and cook, stirring, for 4 to 5 minutes. There will be moisture left in the pan.

4. Mix in the spinach or chard and cook, stirring until barely wilted.

5. When the rice is cooked, add the zucchini-spinach mixture and heat through. Season with salt and pepper. The soup will be thick, so additional broth may be added.

Serves 10.

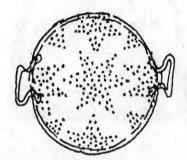

Fresh Mushroom and Brown Rice Soup

A nice variation for this soup is to use barley instead of brown rice. Either one is very nutritious and good for you!

2 tablespoons butter or margarine
1 pound fresh mushrooms, washed and thinly sliced (a food processor is great for this)
1 bunch green onions, thinly sliced
5½ cups beef broth
½ cup uncooked brown rice
½ cup dry white wine
½ teaspoon pepper
½ teaspoon thyme, optional
1½ cups evaporated milk
Salt to taste
Garnish: Chopped green onions

1. Melt butter in large saucepan. Sauté mushrooms and green onions until tender.

2. Add beef broth, brown rice, wine, pepper and thyme. Bring to a boil, reduce heat and simmer, covered, for one hour.

3. Add evaporated milk and heat through. Taste for salt. Garnish with chopped green onions.

Serves 10.

Lentil and Brown Rice Soup

I feel as if I'm eating very healthy when I prepare this soup. The rice and lentils combine to make a complete protein - and of course, the more veggies we eat, the better for us!

12 cups chicken broth
1½ cups lentils, sorted and rinsed
1 cup uncooked brown rice
2 pounds canned tomatoes, drained and chopped,
  juice reserved
3 carrots, sliced
1 onion, chopped
2 cups chopped celery
3 garlic cloves, minced
½ teaspoon basil
½ teaspoon oregano
¼ teaspoon thyme
1 bay leaf
½ cup minced fresh parsley
2 tablespoons cider vinegar, or to taste
Salt and pepper to taste
Garnish: Additional chopped parsley

1. In a large stock pot, combine the broth, lentils, rice, tomatoes, reserved juice, carrots, onion, celery, garlic, basil, oregano, thyme, and bay leaf. Bring to a boil, reduce heat and simmer, covered, stirring occasionally, for 40 to 45 minutes, or until the lentils and rice are tender.

2. Stir in the parsley, vinegar, salt and pepper to taste, and discard the bay leaf. The soup will be thick and will thicken as it stands. Thin the soup, if desired, with additional hot chicken broth or water. Garnish with chopped parsley.

Serves 16 - 18.

Pistou

This is Carol Bade's recipe that dates back to our supper club days. It's a great, inexpensive soup for a crowd — a soup that tastes even better the next day. All you need to add is a crisp green salad and crusty French bread.

8 cups water
1 cup dried white beans, sorted and rinsed
1 16-ounce can tomatoes with juice
1 to 2 tablespoons dried basil or ¼ cup fresh basil
4 garlic cloves, minced
1 tablespoon salt
1 teaspoon black pepper
2 yellow onions, sliced
¼ cup olive oil or salad oil
2 potatoes, peeled and diced
½ pound fresh green beans or 1 (10-ounce) package frozen
   cut green beans
4 cups julienned zucchini
¼ cup chopped parsley
Garnish: Freshly grated Romano cheese

1. In a large stock pot, bring water to boil. Add white beans and boil for 2 minutes. Reduce heat and simmer, covered, for 1 hour, or until tender.

2. Add chopped tomatoes and juice, the basil, garlic, salt and pepper to the beans. Simmer, covered, for 15 minutes.

3. Sauté onions in oil until golden. Add to soup along with potatoes and green beans. Simmer covered for 15 minutes.

4. Add zucchini and cook just until zucchini is tender. Add chopped parsley and adjust seasonings. Garnish with freshly grated Romano cheese. Other good garnishes would be garlic-cheese croutons, additional chopped parsley, or fresh basil pesto.

Serves 10 - 12.

Note: You may need to add more liquid, either water, tomato juice or chicken broth.

Hearty German Potato Soup

Potato soup is always popular in our Tea Room. The addition of sausage in this recipe makes it a real hit — especially with the men!

½ cup vegetable oil
½ cup flour
1 large onion, chopped
1 cup chopped celery
2 teaspoons paprika
8 medium potatoes, peeled and cubed
2 quarts hot water
1 garlic clove, minced
1 pound ham hocks
1 pound cubed ham and/or smoked sausage, optional
1 tablespoon salt
1 teaspoon pepper
1 cup sour cream
Garnish: Additional sour cream, chopped green onions, and
   paprika

1. In a large stock pot, cook vegetable oil and flour until golden brown, making a light roux. Add onion, celery and paprika and cook until vegetables are wilted.

2. Add potatoes and brown slightly.

3. Add hot water, garlic, ham hocks, ham and/or sausage, salt, and pepper. Cover and simmer for 45 to 60 minutes. Carefully remove ham hocks, and allow to cool slightly. Remove meat from bone; cut into cubes.

4. Coarsely mash potatoes with potato masher. Return meat to soup and discard bones. Add the cubed ham and/or sliced sausage. Heat through and stir in sour cream. Garnish with paprika and extra sour cream. Chopped green onions would be pretty too!

Serves 12 - 16.

Parsley-Potato Soup

Don't overlook this one! Everything about this soup is wonderful — it's light, tasty, and nutritious. Just think of the vitamins you're getting from all that parsley.

1½ cups chopped onion
3 tablespoons butter
4 pounds red potatoes, peeled and thickly sliced
8 to 10 cups chicken broth
3 cups finely chopped parsley
2 tablespoons fresh lemon juice
1 teaspoon black pepper, or to taste
Salt to taste
Garnish: Sour cream or yogurt or lemon slices

1. In a large stock pot, sauté onion in butter until just tender.
2. Add potatoes and chicken broth. Cover and bring to a gentle boil. Cook 15 minutes or until potatoes are soft.
3. Purée in blender or coarsely mash potatoes with a potato masher.
4. Add parsley, lemon juice, and pepper. Heat through and taste for salt. Serve immediately - the parsley darkens the longer it is heated. Garnish with dollop of sour cream or yogurt or a lemon slice.

Serves 12.

Leek and Potato Soup

Until we opened the Tea Room I didn't know the efficient way to wash leeks. You may already know - if not, here you are! Slice off the root and the ragged green part. Then slice the whole leek lengthwise - wash under running water, carefully removing all the hidden dirt. To make this a low-fat soup, leave out the butter. Just mix all ingredients in a stock pot and simmer until done. Enjoy guilt-free eating!

3 pounds medium potatoes
3 leeks or about 6 cups chopped
6 tablespoons butter
6 to 8 cups water or chicken broth
1 cup half and half or evaporated milk
Salt and pepper to taste
Garnish: Bacon bits and/or sour cream and chives

1. Peel and cube potatoes. Wash, trim, and chop the leeks, using as much of the green tops as is fresh.

2. In large stock pot, melt butter and add leeks, lightly cooking on medium heat until wilted.

3. Add potatoes and broth. Bring to boil, reduce heat and simmer until potatoes are tender, about 40 to 45 minutes. If a thicker soup is desired, drain some of the liquid at this time. Add half and half or evaporated milk and heat before serving. Taste for salt and pepper. Garnish with bacon bits and/or sour cream.

Serves 14 - 16.

Jalapeño-Potato Soup

This is one of our newest soup recipes and it is proving to be a favorite of our customers. In fact, Gourmet Magazine requested our recipe!

1 medium onion, chopped
¼ cup butter or margarine
5 pounds russet potatoes, peeled and cubed
8 cups chicken broth
1 teaspoon comino
¼ to ½ cup coarsely chopped pickled jalapeños and juice
Pinch of baking soda to prevent curdling
4 cups evaporated milk
Salt and pepper to taste
Garnish: Sour cream and chopped green onions

1. In a large stock pot, sauté onion in butter or margarine until just tender.

2. Add potatoes, chicken broth, and comino. Cover and cook until potatoes are tender, about 20 to 30 minutes.

3. When done, add jalapeños, soda, and evaporated milk. Coarsely mash potatoes with a potato masher.

4. Stir well and taste for salt and pepper. Simmer for 15 minutes, stirring frequently. Garnish with a dollop of sour cream and chopped green onions.

Serves 16 - 18.

Split Pea Soup

For added color and texture, try adding a handful of frozen green peas just before serving. This will add unexpected crunch and interest.

2 cups diced onion
¼ cup butter or margarine
2 cups chopped or sliced celery
2 cups sliced carrots
4 cups split peas, sorted and rinsed
1 or 2 ham hocks (about 1 pound each)
16 cups chicken broth
1 bay leaf
1½ teaspoons black pepper
¼ cup brown sugar
1½ teaspoons thyme
1½ teaspoons marjoram
Salt to taste
Garnish: Sour cream or sherry

1. In a large stock pot, sauté diced onion in butter or margarine. Add celery and carrots and continue cooking for a few minutes.

2. Add the remaining ingredients, and bring to a boil. Reduce heat and simmer, covered, for 2 hours until peas are very soft. Add more liquid as necessary.

3. Remove ham hocks and allow to cool. Remove meat from bone, cut into cubes, and return meat to soup.

4. Carefully purée soup in small batches. (This is an optional step). Serve hot, garnished with sour cream or a drizzle of dry sherry.

Serves 18 - 20.

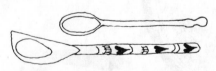
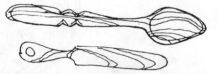

Creamy Zucchini Soup

This is a good summer soup when zucchini is abundant in family gardens. Served hot or cold, your family and friends will really enjoy it.

1 medium onion, chopped
2 tablespoons butter or margarine
3 pounds zucchini, diced
3 carrots, sliced
6 cups chicken broth
16 ounces cream cheese, softened
½ teaspoon nutmeg
1 tablespoon minced pickled jalapeño and juice
Salt and pepper to taste

1. In a stock pot, sauté onion in butter or margarine.

2. Add zucchini, carrots and chicken broth. Cook for 15 to 20 minutes, or until vegetables are just tender. If the zucchini is over-cooked, it will lose its color.

3. Purée half of the zucchini mixture in a blender or food processor. Repeat with remaining half. Be careful when blending hot mixtures.

4. Return puréed mixture to sauce pan. Add cream cheese, nutmeg, jalapeño and juice. Stir over low heat until cream cheese is melted and mixed well. Taste for salt and pepper. Do not overcook. Garnish with additional nutmeg.

Serves 12.

Broccoli Cream Soup

This soup should be served immediately. The broccoli loses its color the longer it is heated.

3 packages (10 ounces each) frozen chopped broccoli (or 1 large bunch fresh broccoli, cut in chunks) Don't forget to peel stems of fresh broccoli and add them too; don't throw away all those vitamins!
1 cup chopped onion
6 cups chicken broth
4 tablespoons butter or margarine
4 tablespoons flour
6 cups half and half or evaporated milk
1 teaspoon white pepper
1 teaspoon dried basil, or 1 to 2 tablespoons fresh
Salt to taste

1. Combine broccoli, onion, and chicken broth in a stock pot. Heat to boiling, reduce heat, and simmer for 5 minutes.

2. Cool slightly and blend until smooth in food processor or blender. Set aside.

3. Melt butter or margarine in same pot; add flour and stir until blended.

4. Add half and half, or evaporated milk, pepper, basil, and puréed vegetable mixture, stirring constantly, until hot and slightly thickened. Taste for salt. This soup is delicious piping hot or well chilled.

Serves 12.

Spinach Bisque

Serve this soup immediately so that the spinach will keep it's bright green color. A delicious variation can be made by adding a 10-ounce can of artichokes and a 4-ounce can of sliced pimentos.

6 tablespoons butter
1 cup chopped onion
6 tablespoons flour
4 cups chicken broth
3 cups evaporated milk
2 10-ounce packages frozen chopped spinach, thawed but not
    drained
Salt and white pepper to taste
Garnish: Grated nutmeg

1. In stock pot, melt butter and sauté onions until tender.

2. Add flour and stir until bubbly. Add chicken broth and milk gradually, stirring to make sauce.

3. Add spinach, and simmer 5 to 10 minutes, stirring to blend. Remove from heat.

4. Purée ½ of soup in blender. Add to remaining soup and heat through. Taste for salt and pepper. Garnish with fresh grated nutmeg.

Serves 8 - 10.

Cheese and Artichoke Soup

This soup came about as a result of two of our favorite flavors! Hector just loves cheese soup and my favorite is artichoke, so I combined the two and the result was most rewarding!

¼ cup butter or margarine
1 cup chopped onions
1 cup sliced carrots
1 cup diced celery
¼ cup flour
1½ tablespoons cornstarch
⅛ teaspoon baking soda (to prevent curdling)
4 cups chicken broth
4 cups milk (or 2 cups water and 2 cups evaporated milk)
2 cups grated extra sharp Cheddar cheese
1 teaspoon black pepper
2 14-ounce cans artichoke hearts, drained and quartered
Salt to taste
Garnish: Additional grated Cheddar cheese, parsley, and
  paprika

1. Melt butter or margarine in a stock pot and sauté onions, carrots, and celery.

2. Combine flour, cornstarch and baking soda, and add to vegetables.

3. Add chicken broth and mix well.

4. Add milk and stir until mixture boils and thickens. Reduce heat and add cheese and pepper. Stir until melted, then add artichokes. Taste for salt. Garnish with additional grated Cheddar cheese, parsley, and paprika.

Serves 12.

Kathleen's
Cream of Artichoke Soup

Kathleen McClellan of Dallas, is our greatest artichoke soup fan. She's been visiting the Tea Room since she was 8 years old. Each time she's in town, she lets us know and we make artichoke soup the "Soup of the Day"!

1 medium onion, finely chopped
2 tablespoons butter or margarine
2 tablespoons flour
2 cups chicken broth
2 14-ounce cans artichoke hearts, rinsed, drained and coarsely
  chopped
1¼ cups evaporated milk
¼ cup chopped parsley
Salt and white pepper to taste
Garnish: Additional parsley, finely chopped

1. In a large stock pot, sauté onion in butter or margarine. Add flour and cook for 2 minutes, stirring constantly.

2. Add chicken broth and artichokes. Cook on medium heat, until mixture thickens, stirring constantly.

3. Carefully purée in blender or food processor. (This step is optional.) Return to stock pot and add milk. Cook on medium heat, stirring for 5 minutes, or until heated through.

4. Add chopped parsley, salt and white pepper to taste. Serve hot or cold. Garnish with additional finely chopped parsley.

Serves 6 - 8.

Peach Tree Cheese Soup

This is a velvety, rich and creamy soup. It is always a popular soup with kids who come into our Tea Room (kids of ALL ages!).

½ cup butter or margarine
1 cup finely diced onion
1 cup thinly sliced carrots
1 cup finely sliced or diced celery
½ cup flour
3 tablespoons cornstarch
8 cups chicken broth
8 cups milk (4 cups evaporated milk and 4 cups water)
1 pound Cheddar cheese, grated
1 pound processed cheese (such as Velveeta), cubed
¼ teaspoon baking soda
2 tablespoons chopped parsley
Salt and pepper to taste
Garnish: Additional parsley and paprika

1. Melt butter or margarine in large stock pot. Sauté vegetables until tender.
2. Stir in flour and cornstarch. Cook for one minute, stirring constantly.
3. Add broth and milk gradually, blending into smooth sauce. Cook over low heat, stirring constantly until thickened.
4. Add soda and cheeses. Stir constantly until cheese is melted.
5. Season with salt and pepper. Add parsley. Garnish with additional chopped parsley and paprika.

Serves 14 - 16.

Note: A trick to shorten cooking time — heat the evaporated milk before adding to the flour, cornstarch, and broth. This speeds the thickening process.

Monterey Jack Cheese Soup

Try this wonderful soup — it's a new and unusual way to prepare cheese soup.

1 cup finely chopped onion
7 tablespoons butter, divided
2 cups chicken broth
½ cup canned chopped green chiles
1 teaspoon chopped garlic
6 tablespoons flour
5 cups milk (or 2½ cups evaporated milk and 2½ cups water)
1 cup peeled, diced tomatoes
3 cups grated Monterey Jack cheese
¼ teaspoon baking soda
Salt and white pepper to taste
Garnish: Chopped parsley

1. In a medium saucepan, sauté chopped onion in 1 tablespoon butter for about 5 minutes. Add the chicken broth, green chiles and garlic. Bring to boil, reduce heat and simmer for 10 minutes.

2. Meanwhile in a large saucepan, melt the remaining 6 tablespoons butter and gradually add flour. Cook over low heat, stirring constantly, for about 2 minutes.

3. Heat milk (or water and evaporated milk), and gradually add to butter-flour mixture. Cook over low heat about 10 minutes until thickened, stirring frequently.

4. Remove broth from heat and gradually add to milk mixture. Add tomatoes, cheese, and soda to prevent curdling. Heat through, stirring constantly. Add salt and pepper to taste. Garnish with chopped parsley.

Serves 8.

David's Favorite Chicken Soup

This is definitely one of our son's very favorite soups! I froze it in small containers for David to take to college. It tastes like chicken in gravy, which is probably why he loves it so much. It's a soup for wintry days, or when you don't feel real chipper. Be sure to serve it with a green salad so you get your veggies!

⅓ cup butter or margarine
¾ cup flour
6½ cups chicken broth, divided
1½ cups warm evaporated milk
1¾ to 2 cups finely diced cooked chicken
¼ teaspoon white pepper
Salt to taste
Garnish: Chopped parsley and paprika

1. Melt butter or margarine; add flour and cook over low heat until well blended.
2. Slowly add 2½ cups chicken broth, constantly stirring with whisk until blended.
3. Cook slowly, stirring frequently, until thick. Add remaining 4 cups of the chicken broth, the warm evaporated milk, chicken and white pepper. Heat just to boiling.
4. Taste for salt. Garnish with parsley and a dash of paprika.

Serves 8 - 10.

Note: A delicious variation would be to add water chestnuts, celery, pimento, carrots, dash of sherry, and top with toasted almonds!!

Chili Blanco

This is an outstanding soup - MY VERY FAVORITE TASTES - all in one bowl!

1 pound (2 cups) Great Northern white beans, sorted and
  soaked overnight in water, then drained
10 cups chicken broth
2 garlic cloves, minced
2 medium onions, chopped, divided
1 tablespoon oil
2 4-ounce cans green chiles, sliced
3 cups canned tomato quarters and juice
2 teaspoons ground comino
1½ teaspoons oregano
¼ teaspoon ground cloves
¼ teaspoon cayenne pepper
4 cups diced cooked chicken
Salt to taste
Garnish: Grated Monterey Jack cheese and chopped green
  onions

1. Combine beans, chicken broth, garlic, and half of the onions in a large pot and bring to a boil. Reduce heat and simmer until the beans are very soft - about 2 hours, or until done. Add more broth as necessary.

2. In a skillet, sauté remaining onions in oil until tender.

3. Add chiles, tomatoes, juice, and seasonings. Mix thoroughly. Add to bean mixture.

4. Add chicken and continue to simmer 1 hour. Taste for salt. Garnish with grated cheese and chopped green onions.

Serves 16.

Santa Fe Corn Soup

This corn soup recipe has all the flavors reminiscent of Santa Fe! The chicken, green chiles and tomatoes give it a very exciting flavor. Serve it with a pretty green salad and flour tortillas the next time you entertain.

3½ cups fresh corn kernels (8 to 12 ears), or frozen corn
1 cup chicken broth
¼ cup butter or margarine
2 cups milk (or 1 cup evaporated milk and 1 cup water)
1 garlic clove, minced
1 teaspoon oregano
Salt and pepper to taste
3 tablespoons canned chiles, rinsed and diced
1 cup cubed cooked chicken
1 cup grated Monterey Jack cheese
¼ teaspoon baking soda
1 cup diced fresh tomatoes
Garnish: Fresh oregano and fried tortilla triangles

1. Combine corn and chicken broth in blender or food processor and purée.

2. In 3-quart saucepan combine butter or margarine and corn mixture and simmer slowly 5 minutes, stirring to keep corn from sticking to bottom of pan. Add milk, garlic, oregano, salt and pepper and bring to boil.

3. Reduce heat, and add chiles and chicken. Simmer 5 minutes.

4. Remove soup from heat and add cheese and baking soda (to prevent curdling). Stir until melted.

5. To serve, ladle soup into 6 bowls. Top with tomatoes and garnish with tortilla triangles and a sprig of fresh oregano.

Serves 6.

Tortilla Soup

Always our SOUP OF THE DAY on Fridays. This South of the Border soup will bring many Olés!

1 chicken (about 3 pounds, excluding liver and gizzards)
5 quarts cold water
1 tablespoon ground comino
½ cup fresh cilantro
1 tablespoon salt
1 large carrot, sliced
3 celery ribs, sliced
1 large onion, chopped
1½ teaspoons coarse pepper
2 garlic cloves
2 teaspoons dried oregano
Garnish: Monterey Jack cheese, lime slices, 3 cups fried
    tortilla strips, 1½ cups chopped avocado

1. Place all ingredients in a large stock pot. Bring to a boil and simmer, covered, for 1½ to 2 hours.
2. Remove chicken from broth. Remove meat from bones, and cut chicken into strips.
3. Strain liquid, discard vegetables, and taste for salt. When ready to serve, add to hot broth:

3 cups diced fresh tomatoes
2 cups chopped green onions
¼ cup fresh chopped cilantro
Meat from chicken

4. Into individual serving bowls, place about 2 tablespoons fried corn tortilla strips and 1 tablespoon chopped avocado. Ladle soup into bowl and garnish with 1 tablespoon grated Monterey Jack cheese and a slice of lime. Serve immediately.

Serves 16 - 18.

New Orleans Chicken Gumbo

½ cup chicken fat or vegetable oil
1 cup flour
½ cup chopped green onion
1 medium yellow onion, chopped
2 cups chopped celery
1 cup chopped green pepper
4 quarts chicken broth
3 cups diced tomatoes, canned or fresh
2 cups fresh or frozen cut okra
5 cups cooked rice
3 cups cubed cooked chicken
Salt and pepper to taste

1. Make a roux by heating the oil or chicken fat in a large stock pot. Blend in flour and cook over low heat, stirring constantly, until brown, about 15 minutes. The darker the roux, the better the flavor. Be careful that it does not burn.

2. When the roux is medium brown, add the green onions, yellow onion, celery, and green pepper. Cook the roux with vegetables for about 5 minutes more.

3. Add the remaining ingredients. Bring to a boil, reduce heat and simmer 20 minutes longer. Taste for salt and pepper.

Serves 24 - 30.

Black Bean Soup

Our secret ingredient is a generous dash of the juice from pickled jalapeños — it adds pizzazz! Many of our customers asked us to call them when we made this soup, so we decided to serve it every Thursday.

4 cups dried black beans, sorted and rinsed
12 cups rich beef broth ‑ enough to cover beans well (You can make your own with instant beef bouillon.)
1 onion chopped
2 garlic cloves, mashed
1 tablespoon comino
3 tablespoons chopped cilantro
1 teaspoon salt or to taste
Garnish: Fried tortilla chips, grated Monterey Jack cheese, chopped green onion, and sliced jalapeños

1. Combine all ingredients in a large stock pot. Cover and cook 3 to 4 hours on low heat until beans are very soft. (This can be done the way we do in our Tea Room kitchen. Use a large crockpot and cook all night on low heat setting.)

2. When beans are done, purée in food processor (Be very careful here, as hot liquid will expand.)

3. Place beans back in pot and thin to desired consistency with extra beef or chicken broth. Taste for salt. (Broths vary in saltiness.) Reheat and serve. Garnish with crispy tortilla chips, grated Monterey Jack cheese, chopped green onion, and jalapeños.

Serves 12 ‑ 16.

Tiffany's Bean Pot Soup

I'll never forget the first time I tasted this soup at Barbara Thomas' home in Comfort, Texas. It was a chilly morning, and we were gathering for Bible study and lunch. This soup was simmering in her kitchen, and I don't think anything has ever smelled more wonderful.

3 cups pinto beans, uncooked
Water
2 cups cubed cooked ham
3 cups tomato juice
4 cups chicken broth
2 onions, chopped
3 garlic cloves, minced
3 tablespoons chopped parsley
½ teaspoon celery seed
½ teaspoon leaf marjoram
¼ teaspoon curry powder
¼ teaspoon ground cloves
4 tablespoons brown sugar
1 tablespoon chili powder
1 teaspoon salt
1 bay leaf
1 teaspoon oregano
½ teaspoon comino
½ teaspoon thyme
½ teaspoon basil
1 cup sherry, optional
Garnish: Chopped green onions

1. Sort, rinse and soak beans overnight. Drain. Place in large stock pot and cover with 8 cups fresh water and bring to boil. Simmer covered for 1 hour.

2. Add remaining ingredients except sherry. Bring to a boil, reduce heat and simmer until beans are tender, about 1 hour. Remove bay leaf.

3. Just before serving, add sherry and heat through. Garnish with chopped green onions.

Serves 16 - 18.

Winter Sausage Soup

Our son, Carlos, loves to eat this soup when he comes in from hunting. It's a flavorful and hearty soup!

2 pounds smoked link sausage, sliced (we use Fredericksburg's own Opa's sausage)
1 medium onion, chopped
2 cups sliced carrots
1 28-ounce can whole tomatoes, chopped and undrained
1 cup chopped celery
4 cups peeled and cubed potatoes
16 cups rich beef broth
1 garlic clove, minced
1 tablespoon brown sugar
1 teaspoon pepper
4 cups shredded cabbage
Salt to taste
Garnish: Chopped parsley

1. In a large stock pot brown sausage. Drain off fat.
2. Add remaining ingredients except cabbage and salt.
3. Bring to a boil, reduce heat and simmer, covered, for 1 hour.
4. Add cabbage and cook for 15 minutes more. Taste for salt.
Garnish with chopped parsley.

Serves 18 - 20.

Italian Eggplant and Bean Soup

If you have eggplant lovers in your family, you will have many devotees after you prepare this terrific soup made with Italian sausage. Just add a green salad, crusty French bread, and a bottle of good Italian red wine. You have the makings of a great evening!

1½ cups Great Northern white, or navy beans, sorted and rinsed
8 cups chicken broth
1 cup chopped leeks, white part only
1 cup chopped yellow onions
2 cups sliced fresh mushrooms
3 tablespoons olive oil
2 bay leaves
1 teaspoon black pepper
½ teaspoon thyme
2 tablespoons chopped fresh parsley
½ teaspoon basil
½ teaspoon oregano
½ teaspoon crushed fennel seeds
½ pound Italian sausage, sliced
1 eggplant (weight approximately 1 pound), peeled, diced and tossed with 4 teaspoons salt
Additional olive oil for sautéing
1 16-ounce can whole tomatoes, chopped, undrained
4 garlic cloves, minced
Extra chicken broth or water as needed
Garnish: Romano cheese

1. Combine beans and chicken broth, and bring to a rapid boil. Reduce heat and simmer, covered, for 1 hour.

2. Sauté leeks, onions, and mushrooms in 3 tablespoons olive oil until just tender. Add to the beans along with bay leaves, pepper, thyme, parsley, basil, oregano, and crushed fennel seeds. Cover and simmer for 1 hour or until beans are tender.

3. Bake sausage slices in a pre-heated 350 degree oven for 20 minutes. Drain and set aside.

4. Place salted eggplant in a colander and drain for 20 minutes, reserving liquid. Sauté eggplant in additional olive oil until lightly browned. Add tomatoes and juice, garlic, additional broth and reserved eggplant liquid. Simmer, covered, for 15 minutes, then combine with the beans. Add sausage and cook slowly, uncovered, for 15 minutes.

Correct seasonings, adding more herbs if necessary. Remove bay leaves. Garnish with grated Romano cheese.

Serves 14 - 16.

Hungarian Goulash Soup

This is a hearty soup for winter days! Add a loaf of dark rye bread and a green salad and enjoy a wonderful feast! This soup is best if made the day before so that all the fat can be removed, and the flavors intensified.

2 large onions, chopped
2 tablespoons oil
2 pounds ground chili meat
3 chopped green peppers
2 tablespoons paprika
2 teaspoons caraway seeds
¼ teaspoon cayenne pepper
8 cups water or beef broth
14½ ounce can tomatoes, diced and undrained
½ cup Burgundy wine
1 teaspoon salt or to taste
3 medium potatoes, peeled and cubed
Garnish: Sour cream

1. In a large stock pot, sauté onion in oil until transparent. Add meat and green pepper, browning well. Drain excess fat.

2. Add remaining ingredients except potatoes and simmer 1 hour until meat is tender.

3. Add potatoes and cook 30 to 45 minutes more. Add more water or beef broth as necessary. Garnish with a dollop of sour cream.

Serves 16.

Helpful Tips On Soups
The Tea Room uses evaporated milk in most of the recipes that require milk and cream. When heated, the evaporated milk does not curdle or separate and withstands constant heat.

Note: Many of our recipes call for fresh cilantro. We buy a case at a time, wash and drain it well. Remove the stems and place one bunch in a plastic bag; then store in freezer. When ready to use, remove the bag from freezer, and hit the bag sharply on the countertop to crush the frozen cilantro. Measure the amount that you need for the recipe. Return the remainder of the cilantro to the freezer. A real time saver!

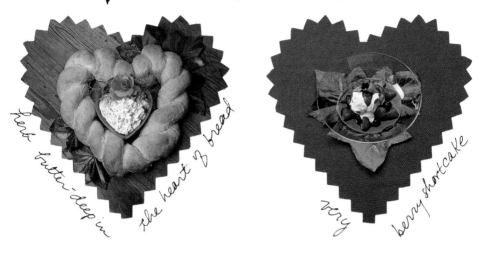

here butter-deep in the heart of bread

very berry shortcake

History, crafts, wildflowers, food — all good things you'll find in Fredericksburg!

Notes

Notes

garden-side tables
in Tea Room.
♥

♥

cynthia's garden
cornucopia for
catering
♥

Great Beginnings
~♡~
Salads

Tomato Aspic

What sets this apart from other aspics is the crunch and texture. It is good served as part of a salad luncheon, with tabouleh, chicken salad, and fruit salad. An assortment of homemade breads and herb butter is a nice addition.

3 tablespoons unflavored gelatin
½ cup chicken broth
4 cups tomato juice
½ cup chopped celery
¼ cup chopped green onion
½ cup chopped green pepper
1 to 2 tablespoons Worcestershire sauce
1 teaspoon celery seed
1 teaspoon salt
½ teaspoon white pepper
1 13-ounce can artichoke hearts, rinsed, drained and chopped
2 tablespoons lemon juice

1. In a small bowl sprinkle gelatin over the cooled chicken broth to soften for 10 minutes.

2. In a non-aluminum saucepan combine tomato juice, celery, green onion, green pepper, Worcestershire sauce, celery seed, salt, and pepper. Simmer the mixture for 5 minutes.

3. Add the softened gelatin and stir the mixture until the gelatin is dissolved. Pour the mixture into a bowl, set in a larger bowl of ice and let the mixture cool, stirring occasionally.

4. Stir in the artichokes and lemon juice. Spray a decorative 1½ quart glass or plastic mold with vegetable coating. Pour in the tomato mixture and chill, covered, for at least 4 hours, or overnight. Unmold onto a lettuce lined platter.

Serves 12.

Note: Great for individual molds also!

Avocado Mousse

This is good with a drizzle of poppyseed dressing and surrounded by fresh fruit. I remember the first time I tasted this at a luncheon at Carol Bade's house — lots of pretty flowers on the table, a chicken casserole, and avocado mousse and fruit. It was years ago, and the delicious impression is still on my tastebuds!

1 6-ounce package lime gelatin
4 cups boiling water
2 tablespoons unflavored gelatin dissolved in ¼ cup cold water
2 cups mashed ripe avocados puréed until very smooth in food processor
1 cup mayonnaise
1 cup heavy cream, whipped

1. Dissolve lime gelatin in boiling water and slowly add dissolved unflavored gelatin. Stir thoroughly until dissolved. Refrigerate until slightly thickened.

2. Purée avocados in food processor until very smooth. Add mayonnaise and blend again.

3. Transfer the avocado mixture to bowl and add whipped cream, gently blending with wire whip. Add thickened gelatin and mix gently but thoroughly.

4. Pour into individual molds or large 3-quart mold that has been coated with vegetable spray. Chill until set and unmold onto lettuce leaves.

Serves approximately 18.

Cranberry and Orange Gelatin Mold

We serve this often when we cater during the Christmas holidays! It's very elegant when unmolded on a silver platter. Garnish with holly, ivy and white mums, for a dramatic effect!

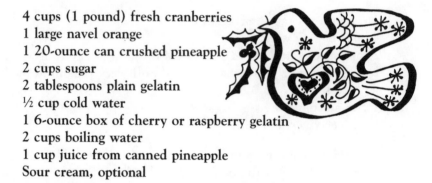

4 cups (1 pound) fresh cranberries
1 large navel orange
1 20-ounce can crushed pineapple
2 cups sugar
2 tablespoons plain gelatin
½ cup cold water
1 6-ounce box of cherry or raspberry gelatin
2 cups boiling water
1 cup juice from canned pineapple
Sour cream, optional

1. Wash cranberries, drain, and process quickly in food processor. Remove cranberries. Add 1 orange, cut in eights, rind and all, to food processor. Process and add to cranberries.

2. Add drained pineapple. Add 2 cups sugar and allow to stand until sugar is dissolved.

3. Dissolve plain gelatin in ½ cup cold water. Dissolve cherry or raspberry gelatin in mixture of boiling water and pineapple juice. Add plain gelatin and stir until dissolved.

4. Chill until slightly congealed. Stir cranberry mixture well and combine with thickened gelatin. Pour into 1½ quart mold that has been sprayed with vegetable coating. Chill until firm, several hours or overnight. Unmold on lettuce lined serving plate. Garnish with sour cream.

Serves approximately 10 - 14.

Cracked Wheat and Parsley Salad (Tabouleh)

This is cool and refreshing in the summer when you have home-grown tomatoes. Cut a large tomato in eighths; don't cut through the base so you can fan it out like flower petals. Serve with a generous scoop of tabouleh and garnish with a lemon slice, parsley sprig, and marigold blossoms. It's delicious and contains fiber! Make extra and keep it in the refrigerator for snacking.

¾ cup cracked wheat (bulgar)
1½ cups chopped parsley
3 medium tomatoes, chopped
⅓ cup chopped green onions (with tops)
2 tablespoons snipped fresh mint or 2 tablespoons crushed
   dried mint
¼ cup olive or vegetable oil
¼ cup lemon juice
1 teaspoon salt
1 teaspoon pepper
Ripe olives, optional

1. Cover cracked wheat with cold water. Let stand 30 minutes. Drain and press out as much water as possible.

2. Place wheat, parsley, tomatoes, green onions and mint in glass or plastic bowl. Mix remaining ingredients. Pour over wheat mixture, and toss well.

3. Cover and refrigerate at least 1 hour. Garnish with ripe olives if desired.

Serves 4 - 6.

Note: For a softer texture, cover cracked wheat with boiling water. Let stand 1 hour.

Cynthia's Jalapeño Potato Salad

In Fredericksburg, we have a Wild Game Dinner annually. We developed this recipe especially for this occasion and it turned out to be a real hit! Since then, we have fixed it often and it always gets raves from the men! It is great with barbeque and baked beans!

10 cups cubed, boiled and peeled potatoes (about 5 pounds)
8 boiled eggs, coarsely chopped
10 ribs celery, diced
10 green onions, chopped
1 large yellow onion, diced
3 to 4 cups good quality mayonnaise
½ cup chopped pickled jalapeños
2 tablespoons juice from jalapeños
¼ cup chopped parsley
2 teaspoons comino
1 tablespoon black pepper
1 tablespoon salt

1. In large bowl, combine potatoes, celery, and both onions.
2. Combine remaining ingredients and add to potato mixture. Mix well and chill several hours or overnight.

Serves 24.

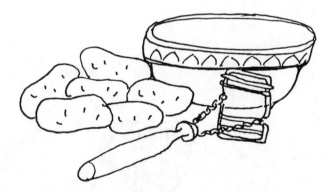

Egg Salad

This outshines any egg salad I've ever tasted because of the texture and the hint of curry flavoring. This filling is a good choice for open-faced tea sandwiches. Garnish with sliced black olives and a sprig of fresh herbs, such as salad burnet, thyme, chives, or parsley.

6 boiled eggs, chopped
2 tablespoons sweet pickle relish
½ teaspoon curry powder
2 tablespoons chopped parsley
¼ teaspoon black pepper
½ teaspoon dill weed
¼ teaspoon dry mustard
1 tablespoon minced yellow onion
1 tablespoon juice from pickled jalapeños
6 tablespoons Peach Tree Herb Mayo (see recipe)

1. Combine all ingredients in bowl. Mix gently until well blended.

Makes 2 cups.

Tuna Salad

This tuna salad is delicious on sandwiches. The ingredients are finely chopped — resulting in a spread that is light and crunchy and tasty. When you make sandwiches, be sure to pile on the alfalfa sprouts!

3 6½-ounce cans water-packed tuna, drained
3 hard boiled eggs, chopped
3 celery ribs, finely chopped
4 green onions, finely chopped
½ cup Peach Tree Herb Mayo (see recipe)
½ cup mayonnaise
½ cup chopped pecans
1 tablespoon sweet pickle relish
¼ cup finely chopped yellow onion

1. Combine all ingredients in a large bowl. Mix gently until well blended. All items can be chopped in a food processor, being careful not to over-process.

Makes approximately 4 cups filling for 8 large sandwiches.

Cynthia's (Really Jo's) Chicken Salad

I learned to make this by watching my Aunt Jo. She would bake two chickens, serve one for supper, and make the other into the best chicken salad I had ever tasted. The single most important part of this recipe, other than the homemade mayonnaise, is the way the chicken is prepared. Whether you use a whole chicken or chicken breasts, the flavor and texture will be better if you salt, pepper, and GENEROUSLY sprinkle the chicken with paprika; then bake at 350 degrees until done.

4 cups cooked, cubed chicken breasts
8 celery ribs, chopped
6 green onions, thinly sliced
¼ finely chopped yellow onion
¼ cup capers, undrained
½ cup Peach Tree Herb Mayo (see recipe)
½ cup Hellmann's (or any good quality) prepared mayonnaise
   (not salad dressing!)

1. Place all ingredients in mixing bowl. Toss lightly until combined. Refrigerate until ready to serve.

Note: This is best if made several hours ahead or the day before to allow flavors to blend.

Makes 6 cups.

Chicken and Rice Salad

This is a Peach Tree adaptation of a recipe from Carol Bade's mother. It's delicious served on a bed of lettuce and makes a spectacular luncheon dish if served in an artichoke or avocado half, garnished with rosemary. Substitute shrimp for the chicken for another great taste treat!

4 cups cooked rice (use while still warm)
1 teaspoon black pepper
½ teaspoon curry powder
½ cup drained and sliced stuffed green olives
1 15-ounce can water chestnuts, drained and sliced
4 celery ribs, sliced
8 green onions, sliced
1 green pepper, diced
¼ cup sliced pimento
4 cups cubed and cooked chicken breasts
2 6½-ounce jars marinated artichoke hearts, coarsely chopped
1 tablespoon lemon juice
¾ cup mayonnaise
¼ cup Peach Tree Herb Mayo (see recipe)
1 tablespoon Balsamic vinegar, optional

1. Combine all ingredients, including the artichoke marinade, in a large bowl and toss gently until well blended.
2. Adjust seasonings. May be served at room temperature, or chilled.

Makes 12 cups.

Jicama and Orange Chicken Salad with Cilantro

This is one of the prettiest of our salads! Sprinkle with violets in the spring. If you are fortunate enough to have a pineapple sage plant, use its bright red blossoms that bloom in late summer.

4½ cups cubed cooked chicken breasts
4½ cups cubed or julienned jicama
2 tablespoons lemon juice
¼ cup orange juice
¼ cup honey
1 garlic clove, minced
¼ cup oil
½ teaspoon black pepper
½ teaspoon salt
2 11-ounce cans mandarin oranges, drained
2 to 4 tablespoons snipped fresh cilantro leaves

1. Combine chicken and jicama in bowl. Set aside.

2. Combine the lemon juice, orange juice, honey, garlic, oil, pepper and salt. Mix well and add to chicken and jicama.

3. Chill mixture several hours or overnight. Before serving, add oranges and cilantro.

Serves 10.

Note: For a pretty variation, add 3 to 4 cups of sugar snap peas!

Green Salad, The Collins Way!

There was a colorful green salad on our table at every evening meal when I was growing up. I continue to serve salads often, and follow the same method I learned at home.

Aunt Jo's Version:

This may appear to be so simple that it's uninteresting, but don't be fooled; it's one of my favorite salads! The more time the oil has to absorb the garlic flavor, the better it will taste!

1. Place mixed greens in medium sized wooden salad bowl.
2. Drizzle 1 to 2 tablespoons garlic-flavored oil over greens. *see below.
3. Add fresh ground pepper, salt, a sprinkle of sugar, and about 1 to 2 teaspoons of fresh lemon juice or vinegar.
4. Toss well and serve.

Serves 4 - 6

Note: Place 2 to 4 garlic cloves in a bottle of salad oil - store in refrigerator for quick salads.

My Mother's Version:

This is the way I learned from my mother. When Tina was little and wanting to be involved in my supper preparations (potentially underfoot!), I would let her stand on a stool and "make the salad." I recommend this to all young mothers - just be sure to tighten the pepper grinder and hand them a slightly clogged salt shaker!

1. Place garlic clove in a wooden bowl and mash with wooden spoon.
2. Add 1 to 2 teaspoons sugar, coarse ground pepper, about ½ teaspoon salt - mix well with mashed garlic.
3. Pour in 2 to 3 tablespoons oil, 1 to 1½ tablespoons vinegar.
4. Stir with wooden spoon to dissolve sugar and salt.
5. Add lettuce and tomato wedges, cucumber slices, radishes, black olives - this is up to you. Toss well and serve.

Serves 4 - 6.

Greek Salad Dressing

1½ teaspoons oregano
1½ teaspoons sugar
1½ teaspoons black pepper
1 teaspoon salt
½ teaspoon minced garlic
1½ teaspoons coarse grain mustard
¼ cup cider vinegar
¼ cup Burgundy wine
¼ cup water
2 tablespoons balsamic vinegar
1½ cups oil (we use canola oil)

1. Combine all ingredients except oil in blender. Blend well.
2. With machine running, slowly add oil until thoroughly blended.

Makes 2½ cups.

Poppy Seed Dressing

Use on the usual fruit salads — and also try tossing it over a salad of fresh spinach and leaf lettuce, strawberries, oranges, avocados, and toasted almonds!

3 tablespoons chopped yellow onion
⅔ cup apple cider vinegar
1½ cups sugar
2 teaspoons dry mustard
2 teaspoons salt
2 cups salad oil
3 tablespoons poppy seeds

1. Using a blender or food processor, mix onion and vinegar, blending until onions are finely chopped.
2. Add sugar, mustard, and salt. Blend again. With machine running, add oil slowly until the mixture thickens.
3. Stir in poppy seeds. Store in refrigerator.

Makes 3½ cups.

Raspberry Vinaigrette

This is the dressing we use on individual green salads topped with fresh strawberries, toasted walnuts and red onions. It's an outstanding way to begin a meal!

1 tablespoon raspberry preserves
1½ teaspoons salt
1½ teaspoons black pepper
¼ teaspoon minced garlic
¾ cup raspberry vinegar
1½ cups oil (we use canola oil)

1. Combine all ingredients except oil in blender. Blend well.
2. With machine running, slowly add oil until thoroughly blended.

Makes 2½ cups.

Peach Tree Herb Mayo

This is the mayo used in our chicken and tuna salads. Fresh herbs can be added when in season.

½ cup fresh parsley sprigs
1 green onion
¼ teaspoon minced garlic
3 eggs
1 tablespoon lemon juice
1½ teaspoons apple cider vinegar
1½ teaspoons whole grain Pommery mustard or Dijon mustard
Dash of Tabasco
1 teaspoon salt
½ teaspoon white pepper
1½ teaspoons dill weed
2¼ cups oil (we use canola oil)

1. Combine all ingredients except oil in a food processor or blender. Process until chopped fine and well blended.
2. With machine running, slowly add oil, allowing the mayo to thicken as the oil is added.

Makes 4 cups.

Love
and
Quiches

I first heard of Quiche Lorraine after my mother's return from a visit to France. I was instantly intrigued and couldn't wait to make one myself! A successful quiche must begin with a light flaky crust! Once you've accomplished that, the filling possibilities are truly limited only by your own imagination. I like quiche because of its versatility — it transports easily for picnics or potlucks.

Consider some of these variations:
* *ratatouille with Swiss cheese or goat cheese
* *asparagus, leek, mushroom with Swiss cheese
* *zucchini, pimento, red onion with Swiss cheese, sliced tomatoes on top and sprinkled with grated Romano cheese
* *add 1½ cups goat cheese in teaspoon size chunks to the chicken zucchini recipe
* *cooked chicken, jalapeños, spinach, goat cheese, Monterey Jack cheese
* *artichokes, red onions, mushrooms, feta cheese, Monterey Jack cheese
* *sautéed onions, potatoes, cooked sausage or bacon, with Cheddar cheese - a great breakfast quiche!
* *sliced cooked chicken breasts, artichoke hearts, green onion tops, and a splash of sherry

Many of our quiche recipes call for clarified butter. Once you use it to sauté you will want to keep it on hand always!

Clarified Butter

1. Place 1 pound of butter (not margarine) in a large pyrex measuring cup. Microwave the butter for 2 minutes on high until melted. This can also be done on the stove in a saucepan, taking care that the butter does not burn.

2. Place the measuring cup in the freezer and freeze until the butter is solid. Using the point of a sharp knife, lift the frozen butter from the measuring cup. Gently rinse the butter solid under cold running water to remove all the foamy milk solids.

3. Blot the butter with paper towels. Cut into smaller chunks, if desired, and store in a plastic bag in the freezer. You may want to cut the block into 1 tablespoon pieces.

The advantage of using clarified butter is that it will not burn when sautéing at high temperatures. It would be time-saving to clarify several pounds of butter at a time.

Basic Quiche Crust

1½ cups unsifted unbleached flour
½ teaspoon salt
2 tablespoons Crisco shortening
6 tablespoons CHILLED butter (not margarine)
5 tablespoons ICED water

1. Mix flour and salt in bowl. Cut in Crisco and butter with a pastry blender until crumbly.
2. Add ICED water, a little at a time, mixing with a fork until well blended. Place dough into plastic bag and gently press dough together into a flat disk. Seal bag. Refrigerate dough for 30 to 60 minutes. This allows the gluten to develop in the dough.
3. On floured board, carefully roll dough to fit quiche pan 10" in diameter by 2" deep. Carefully lift into pan, trimming dough, and rolling edge under to form a rim. Flute the edge.
4. Put a layer of foil over dough and fill to the top with either pie weights or dry pinto beans. This prevents crust from puffing up and shrinking.
5. Bake crust for 15 minutes in a pre-heated 400 degree oven.
6. Remove beans and foil, prick crust bottom with fork several times, and bake 10 more minutes at 400 degrees. The quiche crust is now ready for filling. Reduce temperature of oven to 350 degrees.

Makes 1 quiche crust, 10" diameter x 2" deep.

Chicken in Lemon Pastry Quiche

This is one of my favorite quiche combinations. The hint of lemon in the pastry is delicate and delicious — especially nice for light luncheons and spring brunches!

Lemon Pastry:

Refer to Basic Quiche Crust recipe. When mixing pastry, add zest of one lemon, and replace 2 tablespoons of iced water with 2 table-spoons of lemon juice. Partially bake as directed.

Filling:

1 large onion, chopped
1 tablespoon clarified butter, margarine or cooking oil
10 eggs
½ teaspoon salt
½ teaspoon white pepper
2½ cups evaporated milk
2 cups grated Swiss cheese
1 cup cubed cooked chicken
Fresh tomato slices and grated Romano cheese

1. Sauté chopped onion in clarified butter, margarine or cooking oil.

2. Beat eggs in blender with salt and pepper.

3. Add milk to egg mixture.

4. In prepared crust, place half of the Swiss cheese on bottom. Layer with chicken and sautéed onions, and finish with other half of cheese.

5. Pour egg mixture over layered ingredients.

6. Top with tomato slices and sprinkle with grated Romano cheese.

7. Bake in a pre-heated 350 degree oven for 1 hour and 30 minutes, or until knife inserted in center comes out clean. Allow to cool for 15 minutes for easier slicing.

Serves: 9 - 10.

Texas Quiche

Chicken, green chiles, and a hint of comino, lends a Southwestern flair to this quiche! It's a real favorite with our customers. We garnish it with a dollop of sour cream and a black olive on top.

1 recipe Basic Quiche Crust, 10" X 2", partially baked according to directions.
⅓ cup sliced mushrooms
2 small carrots, sliced thin
1 tablespoon clarified butter, margarine or cooking oil
10 eggs
½ teaspoon white pepper
½ teaspoon salt
1 teaspoon comino
2 teaspoons sliced pickled jalapeños with juice
2½ cups evaporated milk
2 cups grated Monterey Jack cheese
½ cup canned green chiles, drained and sliced into strips
⅔ cup cubed cooked chicken
Garnish: Sour cream and black olives.

1. Sauté mushrooms and carrots in clarified butter, margarine or cooking oil.

2. Beat eggs in blender with white pepper, salt, comino, and jalapeños and juice.

3. Add milk to egg mixture.

4. In prepared crust, place half of the cheese on the bottom. Layer with mushrooms and carrots, green chiles, and chicken. Sprinkle with remaining half of cheese.

5. Pour egg and milk mixture over the layered ingredients, and top with extra green chile strips, if desired.

6. Bake in a pre-heated 350 degree oven for 1 hour and 45 minutes or when knife inserted in center comes out clean.

7. Allow quiche to cool 15 minutes for easier slicing. Garnish each slice with a dollop of sour cream and a black olive.

Serves 9 - 10.

Chicken Zucchini Quiche

1 recipe Basic Quiche Crust, 10" X 2", partially baked
   according to directions.
3 medium zucchini, shredded
1 teaspoon salt
1 medium purple onion, chopped
1 cup sliced fresh mushrooms
1 tablespoon clarified butter, margarine or cooking oil
10 eggs
1 teaspoon white pepper
8 ounces cream cheese, softened
2½ cups evaporated milk
2 cups grated Swiss Cheese
1 cup cubed cooked chicken
Dried crushed basil

1. Place shredded zucchini in colander, sprinkle with salt, and let
stand for 30 minutes. Squeeze excess moisture from zucchini.

2. Sauté onion and mushrooms in clarified butter, margarine or
cooking oil.

3. Beat eggs in blender with white pepper and cream cheese.

4. Add milk to egg mixture.

5. In prepared crust, place half of the Swiss cheese on bottom. Layer
with chicken, mushrooms, onion, and well-drained zucchini. Finish
with other half of cheese.

6. Pour egg mixture over layered ingredients. Sprinkle top with
crushed basil.

7. Bake in a pre-heated 350 degree oven for 1 hour and 30 minutes,
or until knife inserted in center comes out clean. Allow quiche to cool
for 15 minutes for easier slicing.

Serves 9 - 10.

Chicken Broccoli Quiche

1 recipe Basic Quiche Crust, 10" X 2", partially baked
according to directions.
1 10-ounce package frozen chopped broccoli, thawed
12 mushrooms, sliced
1 medium onion, chopped
1 tablespoon clarified butter, margarine or cooking oil
10 eggs
1 teaspoon salt
1 teaspoon white pepper
2½ cups evaporated milk
2 cups grated Swiss cheese
1 cup cubed cooked chicken

1. Remove all moisture from broccoli (Wrap in a clean cotton
towel and squeeze dry).
2. Sauté sliced mushrooms and onion in clarified butter, margarine
or cooking oil.
3. Beat eggs in blender with salt and white pepper.
4. Add milk to egg mixture.
5. In prepared crust, place half of the cheese on bottom. Layer with
the chicken, well drained broccoli, mushrooms, and onion. Finish with
other half of cheese.
6. Pour egg mixture over layered ingredients.
7. Bake in a pre-heated 350 degree oven for 1 hour and 30 minutes,
or until knife inserted in center comes out clean. Allow to cool 15
minutes for easier slicing.

Serves 9 - 10.

Peach Tree Mushroom Quiche

This recipe came to me from two friends - the first was John Phelps (former chef at the Mansion on Turtle Creek in Dallas.) I took one long look at the list of ingredients and tucked it away in a drawer! Then after opening the Tea Room, Trudy Harris gave me the same recipe. This time I tried it - and gratefully so - because it's become a favorite of many of our customers and friends. Notice this is different from other quiches in that it has NO cheese, just lots of mushrooms and flavor!

Mushroom Quiche Crust:
   1½ cups Wheatsworth cracker crumbs
   ½ cup melted butter, not margarine

   1. Combine cracker crumbs and melted butter. Mix well.
   2. Press crumb mixture firmly into bottom of a 10" X 2" quiche pan which has been sprayed with vegetable coating.

Mushroom Quiche Filling:
   2½ pounds sliced fresh mushrooms
   7 green onions, chopped
   ½ cup butter (not margarine)
   1 garlic clove, minced
   3 teaspoons oregano
   3 teaspoons basil
   1 teaspoon salt, divided
   1¼ teaspoons marjoram
   ¾ teaspoon thyme
   ¾ teaspoon dry mustard
   1 tablespoon lemon juice
   7 eggs
   1⅓ cups evaporated milk
   ½ teaspoon white pepper

   1. In stock pot, sauté mushrooms and green onions in butter. Cook for 10 minutes until soft.
   2. Add the garlic, oregano, basil, ½ teaspoon salt, marjoram, thyme, and dry mustard. Simmer for about 10 minutes. Cool and add lemon juice.
   3. Beat eggs in blender with milk and remaining ½ teaspoon salt and white pepper.
   4. Place mushroom mixture in cracker crust. Pour egg mixture over mushrooms.

5. Bake in a pre-heated 350 degree oven for 1 hour or until set. Remove from oven and add topping.

Mushroom Quiche Topping:
    1⅓ cups mayonnaise
    ⅓ cup evaporated milk
    2 teaspoons dry dill weed

1. Combine all topping ingredients. Spread on baked mushroom filling.
2. Return to oven and bake approximately 20 minutes, or until golden. Allow quiche to cool 15 minutes for easier slicing.

Serves 10.

Quiche Lorraine

1 recipe Basic Quiche Crust, 10" X 2", partially baked
    according to directions.
10 eggs
1 teaspoon salt
1 teaspoon white pepper
2½ cups evaporated milk
2 cups grated Swiss cheese
1 cup diced or slivered Canadian bacon
Mushroom slices, Romano cheese, and butter

1. Beat eggs in blender with salt and pepper.
2. Add milk to egg mixture.
3. In prepared crust, place half of the Swiss cheese on the bottom. Top with Canadian bacon and remaining half of cheese.
4. Pour egg mixture over layered ingredients. Arrange mushroom slices on top, dot with butter and sprinkle with Romano cheese.
5. Bake in a pre-heated 350 degree oven for 1 hour and 30 minutes, or until knife inserted in center comes out clean. Allow quiche to cool for 15 minutes for easier slicing.

Serves 9 - 10.

❤•❤•❤•❤•❤•❤
Ham Broccoli Quiche

1 recipe Basic Quiche Crust, 10" X 2", partially baked
   according to directions.
1 10-ounce package frozen broccoli, thawed
10 eggs
½ teaspoon salt
½ teaspoon white pepper
2½ cups evaporated milk
2 cups grated Swiss cheese
2 cups cubed cooked ham
Freshly ground nutmeg

1. Remove all moisture from broccoli. (Wrap in a clean cotton towel and squeeze dry.)

2. Beat eggs in blender with salt and pepper.

3. Add milk to egg mixture.

4. In prepared crust, place half of cheese on bottom. Layer broccoli and ham, and finish with other half of cheese.

5. Pour egg mixture over the layered ingredients. Sprinkle with freshly ground nutmeg.

6. Bake in a pre-heated 350 degree oven for 1 hour and 30 minutes, or until knife inserted in center comes out clean. Allow quiche to cool for 15 minutes for easier slicing.

Serves 9 - 10.

Monterey Quiche

This is our most popular quiche in the Tea Room. These ingredients can't be beat for flavor! I've always been tempted to add some jalapeño slices — try it if you'd like more fire! But, of course, it is close to perfection as it is written. Enjoy!

1 recipe Basic Quiche Crust, 10" X 2", partially baked according to directions.
10 eggs
½ teaspoon salt
½ teaspoon white pepper
¾ teaspoon sliced pickled jalapeño and juice
2½ cups evaporated milk
2 cups grated Monterey Jack cheese
1 cup chopped green onions
1 cup diced or slivered Canadian bacon
1 cup sliced green chiles, drained

1. Beat eggs in blender with salt, white pepper, jalapeños and juice.
2. Add milk to egg mixture.
3. In prepared crust, place half of the Monterey Jack cheese on bottom. Layer with green onions, Canadian bacon, and green chiles, finishing with other half of cheese.
4. Pour egg mixture over layered ingredients.
5. Bake in a pre-heated 350 degree oven for 1 hour and 45 minutes, or until knife inserted in center comes out clean. Allow quiche to cool for 15 minutes for easier slicing.

Serves 9 - 10.

Creamy Zucchini Quiche

Be sure to try this one - the layer of Pommery mustard next to the crust gives a subtle tangy flavor!

1 recipe Basic Quiche Crust, 10" X 2", partially baked
   according to directions
4 cups shredded zucchini
1 teaspoon salt
1 tablespoon Pommery or other coarse ground mustard
3 large mushrooms, sliced
1 tablespoon clarified butter, margarine or cooking oil
10 eggs
1 teaspoon white pepper
½ cup ricotta cheese
8 ounces cream cheese, softened
2½ cups evaporated milk
⅔ cup grated Monterey Jack cheese

1. Place shredded zucchini in a colander, sprinkle with salt, and let stand for 30 minutes. Squeeze excess water from zucchini.

2. Spread mustard on partially baked crust. Prick crust and bake 5 minutes more at 400 degrees.

3. Sauté mushrooms in clarified butter, margarine or cooking oil.

4. Beat eggs in blender with white pepper, ricotta cheese and cream cheese.

5. Add milk to egg mixture.

6. In prepared crust, place half of the Monterey Jack cheese on bottom. Layer with well-drained zucchini and sautéed mushrooms, and finish with other half of cheese.

7. Pour egg mixture over layered ingredients.

8. Bake in a pre-heated 350 degree oven for 1 hour and 45 minutes, or until knife inserted in center comes out clean. Allow quiche to cool for 15 minutes for easier slicing.

Serves 9 - 10.

♥•♥•♥•♥•♥•♥•♥•♥•♥

Veggie Quiche

Try this one as it is - but then also experiment with other vegetable combinations. When I have fresh spinach or chard in the garden, I put a layer of leaves between the layers of cheese and veggies. When served, a pretty green vein is visible on each slice. Also, try adding fresh chopped herbs. This is one of those recipes where the vegetables you have on hand may inspire you to create something new and wonderful!

1 recipe Basic Quiche Crust, 10" X 2", partially baked according to directions.
1 10-ounce package frozen chopped broccoli, thawed
2 small zucchini, sliced
2 medium carrots, sliced
⅓ cup chopped green pepper
½ cup sliced mushrooms
⅓ cup sliced purple onion
1 tablespoon clarified butter, margarine or cooking oil
10 eggs
1 teaspoon salt
1 teaspoon white pepper
1 tablespoon sliced pickled jalapeños and juice
2¼ cups evaporated milk
2 cups grated Swiss cheese
2 tablespoons grated Romano cheese

1. Remove all moisture from broccoli. (Wrap in a clean cotton towel and squeeze dry.)
2. Sauté zucchini, carrots, green pepper, mushrooms, and sliced onion in clarified butter, margarine or cooking oil.
3. Beat eggs in blender with salt, white pepper, and jalapeños and juice.
4. Add milk to egg mixture.
5. In prepared crust, place half of the Swiss cheese on bottom. Layer with the sautéed vegetables and broccoli and finish with the remaining half of cheese.
6. Pour egg mixture over layered ingredients.
7. Sprinkle top with grated Romano cheese.
8. Bake in a pre-heated 350 degree oven for 1 hour and 30 minutes, or until knife inserted in center comes out clean. Allow quiche to cool for 15 minutes for easier slicing.

Serves 9 - 10.

Spinach Ricotta Quiche

This is a light, delicately flavored quiche — wonderful just as it is. A nice variation would be to add crumbled Italian sausage to the filling and sprinkle the top with oregano before baking!

1 recipe Basic Quiche Crust, 10" X 2", partially baked according to directions.
1 10-ounce package frozen chopped spinach, thawed
10 eggs
½ cup ricotta cheese
1 teaspoon salt
1 teaspoon white pepper
2½ cups evaporated milk
2 cups grated Swiss cheese
1 cup chopped green onions
Fresh tomato slices and grated Romano cheese

1. Remove all moisture from spinach. (Wrap in clean cotton towel and squeeze dry).
2. Beat eggs in blender with ricotta, salt and pepper.
3. Add milk to egg mixture.
4. In prepared crust, place half of Swiss cheese on bottom. Layer green onions and spinach over the Swiss cheese. Sprinkle with remaining half of cheese.
5. Pour egg mixture over the layered ingredients.
6. Top with tomato slices and sprinkle with Romano cheese.
7. Bake in a pre-heated 350 degree oven for 1 hour and 30 minutes, or until knife inserted comes out clean. Allow quiche to cool 15 minutes for easier slicing.

Serves 9 - 10.

The Main Event
♡
Entrées

Seafood Crêpes

This recipe is from my Aunt Jo's personal cookbook. For a special occasion, and a romantic meal, serve it with fresh asparagus and hot rolls. Add a bottle of your favorite white wine and invite your best friend over!

½ cup finely chopped onion
½ cup sliced fresh mushrooms
2 tablespoons butter
1 cup cooked shrimp and/or crabmeat
1 cup canned bean sprouts, drained
1 tablespoon snipped chives
¼ cup butter
¼ cup flour
½ teaspoon dry mustard
½ teaspoon salt
¼ teaspoon pepper
2 cups milk
1 cup grated Cheddar cheese
8 Crêpes
½ cup grated Swiss cheese
¼ cup dry bread crumbs

1. Sauté onions and mushrooms in 2 tablespoons butter. Stir in seafood, sprouts, and chives. Set aside.

2. In medium saucepan, melt ¼ cup butter. Whisk in flour, dry mustard, salt and pepper. Gradually add milk. Boil for 1 minute, stirring constantly. Add Cheddar cheese and stir until melted.

3. Stir ½ cup of sauce into seafood mixture. Spread each Crêpe with 2 tablespoons of mixture. Gently roll up and place seam down in ungreased baking dish. Pour remaining sauce over Crêpes. Sprinkle with Swiss cheese and crumbs. Bake in a pre-heated 400 degree oven for 10 minutes, or until heated through.

Makes 8 Crêpes, serves 4.

Crêpes:

2 eggs
2 tablespoons butter, melted
1⅓ cups milk
1 cup flour
½ teaspoon salt

1. Place ingredients in blender in order given. Blend on high speed for 30 seconds. Scrape sides of blender and blend again, about 20 seconds more.

2. The batter may be refrigerated at this point, or used immediately. For each Crêpe, put 2 to 3 tablespoons batter into medium warm, slightly greased 6" to 7" skillet. Tilt to spread the batter evenly to make a thin Crêpe. When Crêpe is light brown, turn and cook on second side.

Makes 12 - 16 Crêpes.

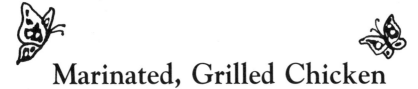

Marinated, Grilled Chicken

You'll find many uses for this chicken. We've used it in sandwiches with jalapeño mayo, sliced into salads, or as the best chicken fajita tacos you have ever tasted! Be sure to make extra to have on hand for next day leftovers.

½ cup dry sherry
2 tablespoons soy sauce
1 to 2 garlic cloves, minced
4 teaspoons sugar
¼ cup oil
6 whole boneless chicken breasts, with skin, cut in half

1. Combine the sherry, soy sauce, garlic, sugar, and oil. Add the chicken breasts to marinade and refrigerate 24 to 48 hours, turning occasionally.

2. Prepare grill. Using tongs, place drained chicken breasts on hot coals. Cook quickly on both sides, being careful not to overcook or chicken will toughen.

3. Using tongs, remove chicken from grill. Remove skin and slice into fajita strips. Serve with warm flour tortillas and fajita condiments.

Serves 10 - 12.

Chilequiles

This Mexican dish is easy to prepare and a real time saver. It is good with or without chicken. To complete the meal, serve a green salad, refried beans, and flour tortillas.

1½ to 2 cups chopped onions
1 cup chopped green pepper
1 garlic clove, minced
2 tablespoons olive oil
6 cups chopped or lightly puréed fresh or canned tomatoes
1 teaspoon pepper
1 teaspoon oregano
Salt to taste
1 10-ounce bag homestyle tortilla chips
4 cups cubed cooked chicken, optional
1½ pounds grated Monterey Jack cheese
Sour cream
Black olives
Cilantro leaves

1. In stock pot, sauté onion, green pepper, and garlic in olive oil until tender. Add tomatoes, pepper, oregano, and salt to taste. Bring to boil, and simmer uncovered for about 10 minutes.

2. In a 10" X 13" baking dish, layer half of chips, all the chicken, half the sauce, and half the cheese. Continue with other half of chips, sauce, and finish with cheese.

3. Bake in a pre-heated 350 degree oven for 40 minutes, until bubbly around edges. Top each serving with sour cream, black olives, and cilantro sprig.

Serves 10.

Variation: Tomatillos Sauce
2 pounds tomatillos, husks removed
2 cups canned sliced green chiles, drained
1½ to 2 cups chopped onions
2 cloves garlic, minced
2 tablespoons olive oil
2 tablespoons butter
⅓ cup flour
2½ cups chicken broth

2 tablespoons chopped cilantro
Salt and pepper to taste

1. Place tomatillos in boiling salted water for about 3 minutes. Drain and coarsely chop tomatillos and green chiles in a food processor.

2. In skillet, sauté onion and garlic in olive oil and butter. Add flour, stirring well. Cook over low heat, about 2 minutes.

3. Add puréed tomatillos and green chiles along with chicken broth to skillet. Simmer uncovered 15 minutes until thickened. Add cilantro, and taste for salt and pepper.

4. Layer as in previous recipe.

Green Chile Strata

This is great as a brunch dish and easy to prepare. It can be assembled the night before for convenience. Serve it with fresh fruit.

6 7½" flour tortillas
4 4-ounce cans chopped or slivered green chiles, drained
½ pound Canadian bacon or ham, cut into slivers
4 cups grated Monterey Jack cheese
5 eggs, beaten
2 cups milk
1 teaspoon salt
Garnish: Green chile strips, optional

1. Generously grease a 9" X 13" baking pan. Cover bottom of baking pan with tortillas, cutting tortillas to fit without overlapping. Sprinkle with half the chopped chiles, half the slivered Canadian bacon or ham, and then half the cheese. Repeat layers, ending with cheese.

2. In medium bowl combine eggs, milk and salt. Pour over the layered ingredients. The top may be decorated with green chile strips. Let stand in refrigerator at least ½ hour or overnight.

3. Bake in pre-heated 350 degree oven for 45 to 60 minutes, or until strata is slightly puffed and bubbly. Cool 5 minutes, then cut into squares.

Serves 10 - 12.

Austrian Chicken Strudel

This is an easy, but elegant way to serve chicken. It always draws raves when we serve it. Garnish each serving with a dollop of sour cream and a fresh rosemary sprig!

4 green onions, finely chopped
⅓ pound fresh mushrooms, sliced
2 tablespoons butter
4 cups cooked cubed chicken
½ teaspoon salt
¼ teaspoon pepper
2 tablespoons chopped parsley
½ teaspoon tarragon
2 eggs, beaten
1½ cups grated Swiss cheese
16 sheets filo pastry
½ cup butter, melted
Garnish: Sour cream

1. Sauté onions and mushrooms in 2 tablespoons butter until tender.

2. In a bowl, combine the onion-mushroom mixture, chicken, salt, pepper, parsley, and tarragon. Stir in eggs and cheese.

3. Lay out 1 sheet of filo pastry and brush with melted butter. Place another sheet of filo pastry on top of the first and brush with butter.

4. Spoon ⅔ cup of chicken filling along one end of the rectangle, leaving a margin of 2" in from the end as well as both sides. Fold in both ends and loosely roll up the strudel. Brush with butter, and place on a greased baking sheet. Repeat this process until filling is used up.

5. Bake in a pre-heated 400 degree oven for 35 minutes, or until crust is golden brown. Garnish with a dollop of sour cream. Each strudel serves 1 person.

Makes 8 strudels.

Chicken Breasts in White Wine

This is a wonderful "company" dish. The chicken will hold up to 1 hour in a 200 degree oven.

6 5-ounce chicken breasts, boned, skinned and lightly
  pounded
3 tablespoons oil
1 garlic clove, minced
1 green onion, sliced
¾ cup dry white wine
¼ pound fresh mushrooms, sliced
1 cup whipping cream
Salt and freshly ground black pepper to taste
1 egg yolk, beaten
1 tablespoon orange zest
Garnish: Additional orange zest

1. Pre-heat oven to 200 degrees. Wash chicken breasts and pat dry. In a skillet over medium heat, heat oil with garlic. Sauté breasts in the oil until browned on both sides, about 5 minutes per side.

2. Remove breasts to an oven-proof serving dish. Keep breasts warm, uncovered, in oven while preparing sauce.

3. Add green onion to drippings in skillet and sauté. Add the wine and simmer until liquid is reduced to about half the original volume. Add mushrooms and quickly heat through. Stir in cream, increase heat to high, and bring to boil to thicken. Reduce heat and season with salt and pepper.

4. Place egg yolk in small bowl. Stir in about ¼ cup of the hot sauce. Pour this mixture back into the skillet and simmer until the sauce thickens. Do not boil or egg yolk will curdle. Add orange zest and simmer briefly, stirring to blend.

5. Pour the sauce over the chicken and serve. Garnish with additional orange zest.

Makes 6 servings.

Pecan Chicken

Every time my good friend, Lucille Salling, comes to visit me in the Tea Room, she brings me a wonderful new recipe. This one in particular was a real winner and I felt I wanted to share it with you!

1 cup flour
1 cup ground pecans
¼ cup sesame seeds
1 tablespoon paprika
1½ teaspoons salt
⅛ teaspoon pepper
1 egg beaten
1 cup buttermilk
8 5-ounce chicken breasts, boned and skinned
⅓ cup butter
¼ cup coarsely chopped pecans

1. Combine first 6 ingredients. Mix together egg and buttermilk. Dip breasts in egg mixture and then coat well in flour mixture.

2. Melt butter in baking dish. Place breasts in dish, turning once to coat with butter.

3. Sprinkle with coarsely chopped pecans. Bake in a pre-heated 350 degree oven for 30 minutes. Do not overcook. Serve with cream sauce, if desired.

Serves 8.

Stuffed Chicken Breasts

This makes a beautiful presentation for a buffet. Accent the sliced spinach-stuffed chicken breasts with a tomato rose and fresh basil. It's also great served warm with a marinara sauce.

1 medium onion, finely chopped
1 tablespoon butter
1 10-ounce package frozen chopped spinach, thawed and
    drained thoroughly
2 cups goat cheese or ricotta cheese
1 egg, slightly beaten
¼ cup chopped parsley
2 cloves garlic, minced
1 tablespoon fresh herbs such as oregano, summer savory,
    thyme, chives
Nutmeg to taste
Salt and freshly ground pepper to taste
1 pound Italian sausage, removed from casing, crumbled and
    sautéed, optional
8 5-ounce chicken breasts, boned with skin left on
Paprika

1. Sauté onion in butter until soft. In a large bowl, combine sautéed onion with rest of the ingredients except the chicken and paprika. Sautéed, drained Italian sausage may be added to the filling ingredients. Mix thoroughly and season well with salt and pepper.

2. Place each breast on a board, skin side up. Trim away excess fat. Loosen skin from 1 side of breast and stuff approximately ⅓ cup of the filling under the skin. Tuck the skin and meat under the breast, forming an even, round, dome shape. Place stuffed breasts in a buttered glass baking dish. Sprinkle generously with paprika.

3. Bake in a pre-heated 350 degree oven for 30 to 35 minutes, or until golden brown. Do not overcook or chicken will be dry. Cool slightly and slice each breast into 3 to 4 slices. Arrange on platters and garnish with herbs and tomato rose. This can also be served at room temperature.

Serves 12.

Chicken Divine

My friend, Frances Worley, brought this to me when I was recovering from an illness. It's an excellent dish - great for parties or covered dish suppers.

1 bunch fresh broccoli
2 cups sliced, cooked chicken breasts
2 10-ounce cans condensed cream of chicken soup
1 cup mayonnaise
1 tablespoon lemon juice
½ to 1 teaspoon curry powder
½ cup grated sharp Cheddar cheese
½ cup soft bread crumbs
1 tablespoon melted butter

1. Cook broccoli until crisp tender. Drain and arrange stalks in shallow, greased baking dish, with flowerets facing outward. Place sliced chicken breast on broccoli.

2. Combine soup, mayonnaise, lemon juice, curry powder and cheese. Pour over broccoli and chicken.

3. Combine bread crumbs and butter and sprinkle on top. Bake in a pre-heated 350 degree oven for 25 to 35 minutes until heated through and bubbly. Don't overcook or the broccoli will turn brown.

Serves 4 - 6.

Chicken Mousse

This mousse can be made the day before. It's a beautiful dish to serve in Spring, garnished with fresh dill. Fresh steamed asparagus is a nice accompaniment. This is great with thinned homemade herb mayonnaise!

1 pound raw boned skinless chicken breasts, cubed
4 eggs
2 garlic cloves, minced
½ cup butter, softened
2 cups cream, half and half, or evaporated milk
1 teaspoon salt
1 teaspoon white pepper
4 green onions, finely chopped
1 tablespoon green peppercorns in brine or capers, drained

1. Place all ingredients except green onions and green peppercorns or capers in bowl of food processor. Process until chicken forms a paste. Stir in green onions and peppercorns, or capers.

2. Place mixture into a greased 6 cup mold or loaf pan and cover with foil. Place dish in a large pan, filled with 1 inch of hot water, and bake mousse in a pre-heated 350 degree oven for about 1 hour until a knife inserted in the center comes out clean.

3. Allow to cool. Cover with plastic wrap and refrigerate. When cold, loosen sides, and unmold onto platter. Spread top with thinned Peach Tree Herb Mayo (see recipe).

Serves 8 - 10.

Chicken Parisienne

This was my first "gourmet" recipe — I received it from my college roommate, Diane. It's failproof, very easy, and most impressive!

6 5-ounce chicken breasts, skinned and boned
1 10-ounce can condensed cream of mushroom soup
1 cup sautéed mushrooms
1 cup sour cream
½ cup sherry
Paprika

1. Place chicken in shallow baking dish.
2. Combine remaining ingredients, except paprika, and pour over chicken. Sprinkle generously with paprika.
3. Bake in a pre-heated 350 degree oven for 45 minutes or until tender. Serve with hot, fluffy rice.

Serves 4 - 6.

Note: This can be assembled the day before it is to be served. Just refrigerate until ready to bake!

Spanakopita

This Greek dish brings applause! The creamy cheese and spinach filling between layers of buttery, flaky pastry makes an impressive dish.

8 ounces feta cheese
4 ounces cream cheese
3 eggs
¼ cup chopped parsley
1 teaspoon nutmeg
1 cup grated Monterey Jack cheese
1 10-ounce package frozen chopped spinach, thawed, drained
 and squeezed dry
1 medium onion, chopped
2 tablespoons butter
½ pound frozen filo leaves, thawed
¾ cup butter, melted
Garnish: Sour cream, dill sprig

1. Combine feta cheese, cream cheese, eggs, parsley, nutmeg, and Monterey Jack cheese in bowl of food processor. Process until well mixed. Stir in spinach.

2. Sauté onion in the 2 tablespoons butter until transparent. Add to spinach mixture. Butter a 9" X 13" glass baking dish.

3. Place 12 filo leaves in the dish, brushing each with melted butter. Spread cheese-spinach mixture over filo leaves. Top with 10 to 15 more filo leaves, brushing each with butter.

4. Cut into squares or diamonds and bake in a pre-heated 350 degree oven for 45 minutes or until brown and crisp. It is important that you cut the spanakopita into serving pieces before baking. Garnish each piece with a dollop of sour cream and sprig of dill.

Makes 8 main dish servings or 16 appetizer portions.

Note: This may be frozen unbaked. Thaw and bake as directed.

Mexican Pizza

This is delicious and makes a striking presentation. Serve it buffet style next to a vase of vibrant zinnias. Accompany it with a green salad, tossed with orange slices, avocados, and rings of red onion. Then, stand back and enjoy the accolades!

½ recipe Cynthia's Famous French Bread dough
3 cups refried black beans (refer to Refried Bean recipe)
1 to 1½ cups goat cheese
¾ cup grated Monterey Jack cheese or Cheddar
Sliced jalapeños
Black olives
Sliced fresh tomatoes
Red pepper strips

1. Gently pat raw dough onto oiled large round pizza pan or rectangular cookie sheet.
2. Top dough with warm refried black beans, gently spreading almost to edge.
3. Crumble goat cheese over beans. Sprinkle with grated Monterey Jack cheese.
4. Arrange remaining ingredients over cheeses. Bake in a pre-heated 375 degree oven for 20 to 30 minutes. Remove from oven and cut in wedges.

Serves 6 as main dish or 10 - 12 as appetizer.

Fredericksburg Game Roll

This is great with Jezebel Sauce or jalapeño jelly.

1 recipe Cynthia's Famous French Bread dough, (see recipe)
½ pound ground pork sausage
½ pound ground venison
2 medium onions, finely chopped
1 10-ounce package frozen chopped spinach, thawed
2 garlic cloves, minced
1 teaspoon dry basil, or 1 tablespoon fresh basil
3 hard-boiled eggs, chopped
⅔ cup grated Romano cheese
Salt and pepper to taste
Cornmeal

1. Prepare yeast dough according to instructions. Allow to rise once.

2. Meanwhile, sauté pork sausage and venison with onion. Drain excess fat.

3. Remove all moisture from thawed spinach. (Wrap in clean cotton towel and squeeze dry.) Add spinach to sausage mixture and mix well. Add remaining ingredients except bread dough and cornmeal. Allow to cool.

4. Divide yeast dough into 4 parts. On a floured surface, pat 1 part of dough into a rectangular shape. Spread ¼ of cooled sausage mixture evenly over dough. Roll up loosely like a jelly roll. Repeat with each remaining part of dough, and the rest of the sausage mixture.

5. Place rolls, seam side down, on a cookie sheet that has been greased and sprinkled with cornmeal. Allow to rise for 15 minutes. Bake in a pre-heated 350 degree oven for 25 to 30 minutes, or until golden.

6. Transfer to wire rack and let cool 10 minutes. Slice and serve warm or cold.

Makes 4 12" rolls. Serves 6 - 8 as a main dish or 18 - 24 as an appetizer.

Corned Beef Brisket

My cookbook would not be complete without this recipe from Charles Schmidt. He's truly one of Fredericksburg's great chefs! We've enjoyed cooking together for many years, especially during our supper club days. Be sure to try this when you can plan ahead. It's definitely worth the effort!!

1 6-pound brisket of beef
4 cups water
1 cup table salt
2 tablespoons saltpeter
½ cup brown sugar
½ cup pickling spice
2 cloves garlic, sliced
2 teaspoons paprika
1 teaspoon whole black peppercorns

1. Place brisket in crock or large non-metallic bowl. Set aside.
2. Combine 4 cups warm water, salt, saltpeter, brown sugar, pickling spice, garlic, paprika, and peppercorns. Pour mixture over beef. Add additional cold water to cover beef.
3. Place a weighted plate on meat to keep it submerged in liquid. Allow to stand in refrigerator for 3 weeks, turning meat occasionally.
4. Remove beef from crock and discard liquid. Transfer the meat to a large stock pot. Add fresh cold water to cover meat. Bring to a boil, and reduce heat, and simmer for 1 hour.
5. Remove beef and discard liquid. Return meat to stock pot, and again add fresh water to cover meat. Bring to a boil, reduce heat, and simmer for 2 hours until meat is tender. Allow beef to cool in liquid. Remove beef from stock pot and trim excess fat. Serve hot or cold.

Serves 16 - 18.

Note: Great in Reuben sandwiches or New England boiled dinner.

Brooke's Hunter Stew

This recipe is from Brooke Schweers - who was the very first Peach Tree Tea Room hostess! Whenever I have a question about venison, I go to Brooke. If you don't have venison, find a friend who does! The first time I prepared this recipe was on a cold Sunday afternoon. The three men in my family were watching football - I offered them a taste and they finished off the pot as a snack!!

1½ pounds boneless venison, cut into ½" cubes
½ pound smoked sausage, cut into ½" slices
2 tablespoons vegetable oil
½ cup chopped onion
½ cup chopped celery
2 28-ounce cans tomatoes, undrained and chopped
1 12-ounce can beer
1 teaspoon salt
1 teaspoon crushed red pepper
1 teaspoon sugar
½ teaspoon rosemary
½ teaspoon basil
½ teaspoon freshly ground pepper
2 carrots, diced
2 medium potatoes, cubed

1. Brown venison and sausage in hot oil in a large stock pot.
2. Add onion and celery and cook until tender.
3. Add remaining ingredients except carrots and potatoes. Cover, reduce heat, and simmer for 30 minutes.
4. Add carrots and cook uncovered for 30 minutes.
5. Add potatoes and cook for an additional 30 minutes or until done.

Serves 6 - 8.

Lasagna

1 recipe Italian tomato sauce
15 ounces ricotta cheese
½ cup grated Romano cheese
2 eggs slightly beaten
1½ teaspoons salt
1 tablespoon chopped parsley
¼ teaspoon pepper
1 10-ounce package frozen chopped spinach, thawed and well
   drained, optional
16 ounces grated mozzarella cheese, or ½ provolone and ½
   mozzarella
1 pound box lasagna noodles, cooked according to package
   directions

1. Prepare sauce. Prepare filling by combining ricotta cheese, Romano, eggs, salt, parsley, and pepper, and optional spinach. Mix well.

2. Spread a thin layer of the sauce in a 9" X 13" pan. Arrange a layer of the noodles, a layer of ricotta filling, a layer of shredded mozzarella, and another layer of sauce.

3. Repeat the layers, ending with a layer of noodles, sauce and mozzarella cheese.

4. Bake in a pre-heated 375 degree oven for 30 to 45 minutes. Remove from oven and allow to cool 15 minutes for easier serving. Cut into squares.

Serves 10 - 12.

Note: An amazing time saver. It's not necessary to cook the noodles first. Layer them as above. It works beautifully and saves time and clean-up!

Italian Tomato Sauce

You will want to keep this Italian tomato sauce handy. In the summer-time when tomatoes are in season, stock up on this sauce and freeze it for use throughout the year! It's a great sauce for pizza, spaghetti, lasagna, and Eggplant Parmesan.

2 cups chopped onions
6 tablespoons olive oil
2 tablespoons minced garlic
1 pound Italian sausage, removed from casing and crumbled
1 pound lean ground beef
8 cups chopped canned tomatoes with juice
2 8-ounce cans tomato sauce
2 tablespoons oregano
2 tablespoons basil
2 bay leaves
4 teaspoons sugar
2 teaspoons salt
Pepper to taste

1. In a large stock pot, sauté onion in the olive oil until soft. Add garlic, sausage, and ground beef. Continue cooking for 3 minutes. Drain excess oil.

2. Add remaining ingredients. Bring to boil. Lower heat and simmer uncovered for about 1 hour.

Makes 10 cups.

Notes

The Added Touch
Side Dishes

Noodles Au Tim

An exciting way to fix noodles. The Tabasco, Worcestershire, and onions makes this a savory side dish.

1 8-ounce package medium noodles
2 cups sour cream
1 cup small curd cottage cheese
1 garlic clove, minced
1 teaspoon Worcestershire sauce
Dash of Tabasco
½ cup chopped onion
¼ cup butter, melted
Salt and pepper to taste
Fresh grated Parmesan cheese

1. Cook noodles according to package directions. Rinse in cold water.

2. Combine all ingredients and pour into a greased casserole dish. Bake in a pre-heated 350 degree oven for 30 to 45 minutes.

3. Top with fresh grated Parmesan cheese.

Curried Fruit

1 29-ounce can sliced peaches, drained
1 20-ounce can pineapple chunks, drained
1 16-ounce can pear halves, drained
1 16-ounce can apricot halves, drained
3 bananas, peeled and cut into chunks, optional
⅓ cup melted butter
¾ cup brown sugar
½ to 1 tablespoon curry powder

1. Combine all fruits in large baking dish.

2. Combine butter, brown sugar and curry powder. Pour over fruits.

3. Bake in uncovered, pre-heated 350 degree oven for 30 to 45 minutes until browned. Additional brown sugar can be sprinkled on top for added crunch. Serve warm.

Serves 8 - 10.

Note: Drained maraschino cherries may also be added for color.

Texas Garlic Cheese Grits

Here is a real crowd pleaser - ideal for hearty brunches and covered dish suppers. It's fast, easy, and freezes well, too!

2 cups uncooked quick grits
8 ounces cream cheese, room temperature
4 cups grated sharp Cheddar cheese
½ cup butter
2 eggs, beaten
4 garlic cloves, minced
1 teaspoon Tabasco
1 teaspoon Worcestershire sauce
2 tablespoons pickled jalapeño slices and juice
Paprika

1. Cook grits according to package instructions.

2. Add cream cheese to hot cooked grits. Stir well and add Cheddar cheese and butter. Stir until melted.

3. Add remaining ingredients except paprika. Pour into large shallow casserole dish. Sprinkle with paprika. Bake in a pre-heated 350 degree oven for 30 minutes.

Serves 12.

Note: May be made a day ahead and heated at serving time.

Mexican Rice

Serve this with any Mexican entrée. It's really good and very different from other recipes that contain tomato.

1 cup raw long-grain white rice
3 tablespoons olive oil
½ cup chopped onion
1 large clove garlic, minced
2 tablespoons chopped parsley
2½ cups rich chicken broth
1 teaspoon salt
1 pickled jalapeño, chopped

1. In saucepan, brown rice in oil together with onion and garlic. Cook and stir until light brown.
2. Add remaining ingredients. Cover and simmer for 25 minutes. DON'T LIFT LID DURING COOKING!

Serves 4.

Refried Beans

3 slices bacon, chopped
3 cups cooked pinto or black beans with some juice (refer to Black Bean Soup recipe for cooking beans)

1. Sauté bacon in heavy skillet.
2. Mash beans. This can be done in a food processor. Be careful not to overprocess.
3. Add mashed beans to skillet, along with bacon and drippings. Cook over low heat, stirring frequently, for 30 to 45 minutes, until thick.

Makes 4 - 6 servings.

Granny Mime's Baked Beans

This is my mother's recipe for really delicious baked beans — they always receive raves at potluck suppers and family parties! This is a tasty dish — excellent on gourmet picnics!

1 53-ounce can pork and beans
½ cup molasses
¼ cup ketchup
¼ cup prepared mustard
¼ cup brown sugar
½ pound bacon

1. Combine all ingredients, except bacon. Place in shallow baking dish and top with bacon strips, cut to fit.
2. Bake in pre-heated 350 degree oven for 1 to 1½ hours. Serve hot or warm.

Serves 8.

Mac and Cheese

I never liked macaroni and cheese until I tried this version. It's light and very tasty. Serve it with a fruit salad and rolls. For variety mix in drained tuna.

1 12-ounce package small elbow macaroni
1 egg, slightly beaten
16 ounces small curd cottage cheese
1 cup sour cream
3 tablespoons chopped onion
1 teaspoon salt
¼ teaspoon pepper
¼ cup chopped pimentos, drained
8 ounces grated Cheddar cheese

1. Cook macaroni according to package directions. Drain and set aside.
2. Combine remaining ingredients and add to cooked macaroni. Pour into greased casserole dish and bake in a pre-heated 350 degree oven for 30 to 40 minutes.

Serves 8 - 10.

Ratatouille

½ cup olive oil
4 cups peeled and cubed eggplant
4 cups sliced zucchini
½ cup green pepper strips
½ cup sweet red pepper strips
½ cup sliced onion
2 tablespoons garlic, minced
½ cup white wine
4 cups chopped tomatoes, fresh or canned
1 teaspoon thyme
4 bay leaves
1 teaspoon basil
1 teaspoon rosemary
1 tablespoon salt
1 teaspoon pepper
1 cup black olives, cut in halves
½ cup chopped parsley

1. In large skillet or stock pot, sauté eggplant and zucchini in olive oil for 8 minutes.

2. Add red and green peppers, onion and garlic. Sauté for 6 minutes.

3. Add remaining ingredients. Place in oven-proof dish and bake in a pre-heated 350 degree oven for 45 minutes. Serve warm or cold.

Serves 10.

Note: Even better the second day!

Bread
and
Breakfast

Biscuits

2 cups flour
1 tablespoon baking powder
½ teaspoon salt
¼ cup chilled butter
⅔ cup milk

1. Combine flour, baking powder, and salt in medium bowl. Cut in chilled butter with a pastry blender until the consistency of coarse meal.

2. Add milk and stir quickly so dough just holds together. Do not overmix. Turn dough onto lightly floured surface and knead lightly, not more than 10 times.

3. Pat dough to ½" thickness and cut with a 2" biscuit cutter. (I use a heart-shaped cutter.) Bake on ungreased baking sheet in a pre-heated 450 degree oven for 12 to 15 minutes.

Makes 12 biscuits.

Ottis' Cornbread

Ottis Layne's cornbread is a recipe that everyone should have in their file. It cooks fast! I make and serve it in my cast iron skillet!

2 cups white corn meal
¼ cup flour (unbleached or whole wheat)
1 teaspoon salt
2 teaspoons baking powder
¼ teaspoon baking soda
1 egg, beaten
2 cups buttermilk
2 tablespoons butter, melted

1. Combine first 5 ingredients in bowl.

2. Combine egg and buttermilk. Add to dry ingredients.

3. Heat butter in oven-proof 10" skillet. Pour batter into sizzling hot skillet. Bake in a pre-heated 450 degree oven for 20 minutes or until well-browned. Slice into wedges, and serve with butter.

Serves 6 - 8.

Quick Bread

My friend, Gail, is one of the best cooks I know. She and I used to bake all our own breads with fresh ground flour when our children were small. This is a healthful bread that is sure to be a hearty addition to any meal!

⅔ cup cornmeal
¾ cup whole wheat flour
2½ teaspoons baking powder
½ teaspoon salt
1 cup milk
1 egg
3 tablespoons oil
3 tablespoons molasses or honey

1. Combine first 4 ingredients. Using a wooden spoon, combine remaining ingredients and add to flour mixture. Mix only until blended.
2. Bake in a greased loaf pan in a pre-heated 425 degree oven for 20 minutes.

Oatmeal Muffins

½ cup melted butter or oil
2 eggs
1 cup mashed ripe bananas
½ cup warm honey
¼ cup yogurt or buttermilk
1 teaspoon baking soda
1½ cups whole wheat flour
¾ teaspoon salt
1 cup quick oats

1. Using a wooden spoon, combine first 4 ingredients. Add yogurt or buttermilk and soda and mix well.
2. Combine flour, salt, and oats. Add to banana mixture.
3. Spoon into greased muffin tins. Bake in a pre-heated 375 degree oven for 18 to 20 minutes.

Makes 12 - 18 muffins.

Blueberry Muffins

I was never impressed with blueberry muffins - I'd always had the kind made with canned blueberries. Then I tried this recipe and used large fresh berries. As far as I am concerned, this is the only way to make them. For a nice change, use dewberries or just a mixture of berries.

3 cups flour
½ cup brown sugar
½ cup granulated sugar
1 tablespoon baking powder
1 teaspoon salt
½ cup melted butter or margarine
3 large eggs
1 cup milk
1½ cups blueberries, fresh or frozen

1. Mix flour, sugars, baking powder and salt in bowl.

2. Combine melted butter, eggs, and milk, and stir by hand into dry ingredients until just blended.

3. Fold in berries lightly and carefully.

4. Spoon into greased muffin tins until they are ⅔ full. Bake in a pre-heated 400 degree oven for 20 minutes or until browned.

Makes 18 medium sized muffins.

Note: For mini-muffins, do not mix in berries. After spooning batter into muffin tins, press 2 to 3 berries into each muffin and bake for 10 to 12 minutes.

Angel Biscuits

On holiday mornings, my family always enjoys a late brunch. I traditionally fix these Angel Biscuits with scrambled eggs and bacon. With my hungry bunch I seldom have any of these left. This dough may be prepared the day before, placed in a large bowl, and sealed well with plastic wrap.

1 tablespoon active dry yeast
2 tablespoons lukewarm water
5 cups unbleached flour (or 4 cups white and 1 cup whole wheat)
¼ cup sugar
3 teaspoons baking powder
1 teaspoon baking soda
1 teaspoon salt
1 cup Crisco shortening
2 cups buttermilk

1. Dissolve the yeast in warm water. Set aside.

2. Combine the flour, sugar, baking powder, soda and salt in a large bowl. Cut in the shortening with a pastry cutter.

3. Add the buttermilk and yeast mixture. Mix well with wooden spoon. Turn onto floured board and knead gently, about 10 times.

4. Roll dough to ½" thickness and cut with biscuit cutter. Place biscuits on an ungreased cookie sheet. Bake in a pre-heated 400 degree oven for 15 minutes.

Makes 24 3" rolls.

Tea Room Variation:
Roll dough into large rectangle. Mix the following ingredients together and spread over dough:

3 tablespoons butter
1 cup brown sugar
⅔ cup chopped walnuts or pecans
⅓ cup currants
1 teaspoon cinnamon

Carefully roll up and cut across making 1 inch rolls. Bake in a pre-heated 400 degree oven for 20 minutes. While still warm, drizzle the tops of the rolls with a mixture of 2 cups powdered sugar and 4 to 6 tablespoons of milk.

Blueberry-Orange Nut Bread

We enjoy breakfast breads and this one is especially good for continental breakfasts. It's quick and easy.

3 cups flour
1 tablespoon baking powder
¼ teaspoon baking soda
½ cup sugar
1 teaspoon salt
3 large eggs
½ cup milk
½ cup butter, melted
1 tablespoon orange zest
⅓ cup orange juice
1 cup blueberries, fresh or frozen
1 cup chopped nuts

1. Combine the flour, baking powder, soda, sugar, and salt.

2. Using a wooden spoon, beat the eggs, milk, melted butter, orange zest, and orange juice.

3. Pour into the dry ingredients and stir until the flour is thoroughly moistened. Add the blueberries and nuts. Stir thoroughly but gently.

4. Pour into a well-buttered loaf pan and set aside for 15 minutes.

5. Bake in a pre-heated 350 degree oven for 1 hour 15 minutes, or until loaf tests done.

Makes 1 large loaf.

Banana Apricot Nut Bread

After trying this version, I don't fix plain banana-nut bread anymore.
The apricots in this recipe are a tart and tasty addition.

½ cup butter
⅓ cup brown sugar
⅓ cup granulated sugar
2 large eggs
1 cup unbleached flour
1 cup whole wheat flour
½ teaspoon salt
½ teaspoon baking soda
1½ cups mashed bananas
½ cup chopped walnuts or pecans
1 cup minced dried apricots

1. Using an electric mixer, cream the butter and both sugars.
2. Add the eggs and beat well.
3. Combine the unbleached flour, the whole wheat flour, salt and soda. Stir into creamed mixture alternating with the mashed bananas. Stir in nuts and apricots.
4. Pour into a buttered loaf pan and let stand at room temperature for 20 minutes. Bake in a pre-heated 350 degree oven for 1 hour and 15 minutes.

Makes 1 loaf.

Back of the loaf — the sun, the wheat, the showers — and the father's will

Whole Wheat Pancakes

Sunday morning wouldn't be complete without pancakes in our house. Some of us like blueberry pancakes, so I add berries at the time I pour in the batter - then everyone is happy!

1 cup whole wheat flour
1 cup unbleached flour
½ teaspoon salt
¼ teaspoon soda
2 teaspoons baking powder
1 cup buttermilk (or yogurt)
1 cup skim milk
2 large eggs (or 3 medium)
Oil

1. Combine first 5 ingredients in bowl. Add the buttermilk, skim milk and eggs, and stir only until mixed. The batter will be lumpy.

2. Heat a small amount of oil in skillet or griddle until a drop of water sizzles on it. Pour batter into pan, making pancakes about 3½" diameter. Cook over medium heat until bubbles appear on top. Flip pancakes over and continue cooking until golden. Serve immediately with butter and maple syrup.

Cynthia's French Toast

This is our son David's favorite breakfast. It alternates with whole wheat pancakes as our Sunday morning breakfast tradition!

1 loaf day-old French bread (preferably Cynthia's Famous French Bread, see recipe)
½ cup milk
6 eggs, beaten
2 teaspoons vanilla
Oil
Powdered sugar

1. Slice bread into ½" slices.

2. Combine milk, eggs and vanilla in shallow bowl. Soak bread slices in milk mixture until soggy.

3. Heat ¼" oil in skillet. Fry toast until golden on both sides. Sprinkle with powdered sugar. Serve with maple syrup and fresh fruit.

Serves 4 - 6.

Puff Pancakes

This is a favorite of my children. When they were small, they liked to watch through the glass window of my oven to see how much the pancakes would puff each time. As Tina became old enough to cook, the boys would ask her to make these pancakes for Saturday morning breakfast while they watched cartoons.

6 eggs
2¼ cups milk
2¼ cups flour
¾ teaspoon salt

1. Place eggs and milk in blender. Blend for 30 seconds on high.
2. Add flour and salt to egg-milk mixture. Blend again, scraping down sides, until thoroughly mixed.
3. Lightly grease three 9" pie pans. Divide batter evenly into pans and bake in a pre-heated 450 degree oven for 12 to 15 minutes until puffed and golden brown around edges. Serve with butter, syrup and fresh fruit.

Serves 4 - 6.

Waffles

These are so good you won't want to limit them just to breakfast. You can serve them at night with venison sausage. Ours is provided by Carlos — the mighty Pedregon family hunter!

2 cups flour
1 tablespoon baking powder
½ teaspoon baking soda
1 teaspoon salt
1½ cups buttermilk or yogurt
3 large eggs
½ cup melted butter
⅔ cup chopped nuts, optional

1. Combine flour, baking powder, soda and salt in bowl. Stir in buttermilk and eggs, beating with spoon until smooth.
2. Add melted butter and optional nuts. Blend well. Allow batter to rest for at least 1 hour, or it can be refrigerated overnight. Bake in prepared waffle iron.

Serves 4 - 6.

Judy's Granola

4 cups rolled oats
¼ cup canola oil
2 tablespoons honey
2 tablespoons molasses
1 teaspoon maple flavoring
1 teaspoon vanilla
¼ cup raw unsalted sunflower seeds
¼ cup raw unsalted pumpkin seeds
½ cup roasted unsalted peanuts
½ cup raisins

1. Combine oats and oil in large bowl. Mix thoroughly.

2. Combine honey and molasses in small bowl. Stir in maple flavoring and vanilla. Add to oats and mix thoroughly.

3. Add all remaining ingredients, except raisins. Bake in shallow pan in a pre-heated 300 degree oven for 40 minutes, stirring occasionally. Allow to cool completely. Add raisins. Store in airtight container in refrigerator.

Makes 5½ cups.

Note: I have two good friends who make their own granola. Each recipe makes breakfast a special occasion. Granola keeps well in the refrigerator and makes a great snack - it's also great on yogurt or mixed into oatmeal cookie dough!

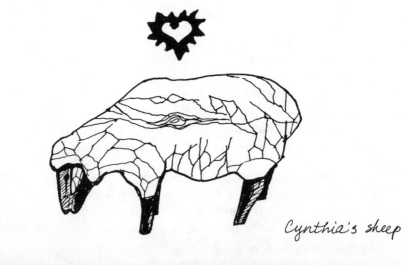

Cynthia's sheep

Cynthia's Flour Child + Enid's newly-wed Plate

Notes

Sally's Granola

Don't think of eating this one when you're dieting. However, it is nutritious if you'd like to have it on hand for the kid's breakfast or snacks!

3 cups rolled oats
1 cup coconut
½ cup wheat germ
½ cup wheat bran
1½ to 2 cups chopped nuts and seeds (Try a combination of
    cashews, walnuts, sunflower seeds, and almonds. You really
    can't go wrong!)
1 cup honey
¾ cup oil
1 tablespoon vanilla
2 cups raisins

1. Combine first 5 ingredients in a large bowl.
2. In small bowl, combine honey, oil and vanilla.
3. Toss with oat-nut mixture, coating thoroughly. Place in large shallow pan and bake in a pre-heated 300 to 325 degree oven for 45 to 60 minutes, stirring every 10 minutes. Add raisins. Allow to cool and refrigerate in airtight containers.

Makes 9 cups.

Refrigerator Yeast Rolls

2 tablespoons active dry yeast
⅓ cup very warm water
½ cup butter
1 cup milk
4¼ to 4¾ cups unsifted unbleached flour, divided
⅓ cup sugar
2 teaspoons salt
3 large eggs, room temperature
Oil
Melted butter

1. Dissolve yeast in warm water. Set aside. In small saucepan over low heat, melt butter in milk.

2. In large bowl, combine 2¾ cups flour, sugar, salt, eggs, dissolved yeast and warm milk-butter mixture. Beat with wooden spoon for about 3 minutes. (This step can be done in a food processor using a plastic blade.)

3. Add remaining flour by hand. The dough will be soft and sticky. Place in an oiled bowl and cover with plastic wrap. Refrigerate several hours or overnight.

4. Turn dough onto generously floured surface. Pat dough to ½" thickness. Cut with a 2" round cutter. Place on ungreased cookie sheet about 1" apart. Brush generously with melted butter.

5. Allow rolls to rise at room temperature about 45 minutes to 1 hour. Bake in a pre-heated 400 degree oven for 10 minutes.

Makes 24 rolls.

Cynthia's Famous French Bread

In our Tea Room, we serve this bread daily. We also use this recipe for our heart shaped breads. When baked in the heart pans, the recipe still makes 2 loaves, only denser.

1 tablespoon active dry yeast
1½ teaspoons sugar
1½ cups lukewarm water
3 cups unsifted unbleached flour
1 cup unsifted whole wheat flour
1½ teaspoons salt
Oil
Cornmeal

1. Dissolve the yeast and sugar in the lukewarm water.
2. Combine the flours and salt. Add to the yeast mixture, stirring well with wooden spoon. (This step can also be done in a food processor using a dough blade.)
3. Knead the dough on a slightly floured board until it is no longer sticky. Place the dough in an oiled bowl; brush top of dough with oil also. Cover, and let rise until doubled, about one hour.
4. After dough has doubled in size, punch it down and turn it out onto floured board. Divide into 2 parts. Shape each part into a long narrow loaf.
5. Place the loaves on a greased cookie sheet that has been sprinkled with cornmeal. Cover, and let rise about 30 minutes. Using a serrated knife, make shallow diagonal slices on top of each loaf. Bake in a pre-heated 400 degree oven for 20 to 25 minutes or until golden.

Makes 2 large loaves.

Pumpernickel Bread with Currants

We bake this bread in heart-shaped loaf pans for serving with our salads in the Tea Room. This bread is also delicious with cream cheese or with thinly sliced peppered ham for special events.

1½ cups lukewarm water
½ cup molasses
1 tablespoon active dry yeast
1 tablespoon instant coffee granules
1 tablespoon salt
1½ tablespoons cocoa
1½ cups unsifted medium rye flour
1½ cups unsifted whole wheat flour
1½ cups unsifted unbleached flour
Oil
1 cup currants
Cornmeal

1. Combine lukewarm water, molasses, yeast, instant coffee granules, salt and cocoa. Stir and let stand for 5 to 10 minutes, or until foamy.

2. Combine rye flour, whole wheat and unbleached flour in a large bowl. Gradually add yeast-molasses mixture, stirring well.

3. Turn onto lightly floured board. Sprinkle the dough with additional unbleached flour and begin to knead. Continue to knead, adding the flour until the dough is smooth and elastic.

4. Form the dough into a large ball, and place the dough in an oiled bowl. Turn the ball of dough to coat with oil. Cover with towel, and let rise until doubled in size, about 1 hour.

5. Turn dough onto lightly floured board. Flatten it into a large rectangle and sprinkle with the currants. Roll up the dough and knead it to distribute the currants evenly, for about 5 minutes.

6. Sprinkle a large greased baking sheet with white cornmeal. Turn the dough out, cut it into 3 pieces, and shape each piece into a small round or oval loaf. Set loaves on the baking sheet, leaving as much room as possible between them, cover, and let rise until doubled, about 30 minutes.

7. Bake on the middle rack in a pre-heated 400 degree oven for 35 to 40 minutes or until the loaves are dark brown, and sound hollow when bottoms are rapped. Cool completely on racks before cutting.

Makes 3 loaves.

Whole Wheat Walnut Bread

2 tablespoons active dry yeast
3 cups warm water
2 tablespoons sorghum syrup, molasses or honey
1 cup unsifted unbleached flour
5½ to 6½ cups unsifted whole wheat flour, divided
3 tablespoons walnut oil
1 tablespoon salt
Additional oil
1 cup chopped walnuts
1 egg plus 1 tablespoon milk or water, beaten for egg wash
Cornmeal

1. Dissolve the yeast in the water in a large bowl. Stir in sorghum syrup, molasses or honey, unbleached flour, and 2 cups of the whole wheat flour. Beat vigorously with a wooden spoon to form a thick smooth batter. Cover and let rise in a warm place for 40 minutes.

2. Stir in the oil and salt. Stir in 3½ cups whole wheat flour, ½ cup at a time. Turn onto floured board. Knead for 5 to 8 minutes, adding more whole wheat flour, only if necessary, until dough is smooth and elastic.

3. Place the dough in an oiled bowl. Turn the dough to coat with oil, cover and let rise until double, about 45 to 60 minutes.

4. Turn dough onto lightly floured board, flatten the dough into a large rectangle. Sprinkle with the chopped walnuts. Roll up the dough and knead for 1 to 2 minutes to distribute the walnuts.

5. Divide the dough into 2 parts. Shape into 2 loaves and place on greased cookie sheets that have been sprinkled with cornmeal. Cover and let rise until doubled, about 30 minutes.

6. Brush tops of loaves with egg wash, if desired. Using a serrated knife, make shallow diagonal slashes on top of loaves. Bake in a preheated 400 degree oven for about 25 to 35 minutes, or until golden brown. Cool on wire rack.

Makes 2 loaves.

German Beer Rye Bread

1¾ cups beer, room temperature
½ cup warmed molasses
2 tablespoons active dry yeast, dissolved in ¼ cup warm water
2 teaspoons salt
3 cups unsifted medium rye flour
3 cups unsifted unbleached flour
1 tablespoon caraway seeds
Oil
Cornmeal
Melted butter

1. In a large bowl, combine the beer and the molasses. Add the dissolved yeast.

2. Add the rest of the ingredients, except the oil, cornmeal, and butter. Blend well, using a wooden spoon. (This step can also done in a food processor using a dough blade.)

3. Turn dough onto floured board. Knead about 7 minutes, using more unbleached flour as necessary to keep dough from sticking.

4. Place the dough in a bowl that has been coated with oil. Brush the top of the dough with oil also. Cover and let rise in a warm place until doubled, about 1 hour.

5. Punch dough down and turn onto floured board. Shape into two oval loaves and place on greased cookie sheets which have been sprinkled with cornmeal. Cover and let rise until doubled, about 30 to 45 minutes.

6. Brush tops of loaves with melted butter. Using a serrated knife, make shallow diagonal slashes on top of loaves. Bake in a pre-heated 400 degree oven for 30 minutes until done.

Makes 2 large loaves.

Dark Rye Bread

2 cups unsifted medium rye flour
¼ cup cocoa
2 tablespoons active dry yeast
1½ cups warm water, divided
½ cup dark molasses
2 teaspoons salt
2 tablespoons caraway seeds
2 tablespoons butter, softened
2½ cups unsifted unbleached flour, or whole wheat flour, or a
   combination of both
Oil
Cornmeal

1. Combine the rye flour and cocoa. Set aside. Dissolve the yeast in
½ cup warm water.

2. Combine the molasses, remaining 1 cup of warm water, salt, and
caraway seeds in a large bowl. Add the rye flour and cocoa, yeast
mixture, the butter, and 1 cup of the unbleached or whole wheat flour.
Beat with a wooden spoon until dough is smooth.

3. Sprinkle the remaining 1½ cups flour on a bread board. Turn
dough onto board, and knead flour into dough. Add more flour, if
necessary, kneading until dough is smooth and elastic.

4. Place dough into oiled bowl; brush top of dough with oil also.
Cover, and let rise in a warm place until doubled, about 1 hour.

5. Punch dough down, shape into a round loaf, and place on greased
cookie sheet that has been sprinkled with cornmeal. Let rise until
doubled, about 30 to 45 minutes.

6. Using a serrated knife, make shallow diagonal slashes on top of
loaf. Bake in a pre-heated 400 degree oven for 30 minutes.

Makes 1 loaf.

Cynthia's Health-Nut Bread

4 cups unsifted whole wheat flour, divided
1½ tablespoons active dry yeast
1½ cups warm water
¼ cup sorghum syrup or molasses
½ cup chopped raw sunflower seeds
½ cup currants
2 teaspoons salt
2 cups oat bran or finely chopped oats
2 cups skim milk, scalded and cooled
3 cups unsifted unbleached flour
Oil
Melted butter

1. In large bowl, combine 2 cups whole wheat flour, yeast, water, and sorghum syrup or molasses. Mix well and cover with plastic wrap. Let set for at least 2 to 3 hours, or overnight, until a spongy dough forms. Do not refrigerate.

2. Combine seeds, currants, salt, oat bran, and skim milk. Add to flour-yeast mixture and mix well.

3. Add the unbleached flour and the remaining 2 cups whole wheat flour. Mix well and turn onto floured board. Knead for 10 minutes until smooth and elastic, adding more flour as needed to prevent sticking.

4. Form dough into large ball. Place dough in oiled bowl and turn the ball of dough to coat with oil. Cover with towel and let rise until doubled in size, about 1 hour.

5. Turn onto floured board. Divide dough into 2 parts, form into loaves, and place each in greased bread pan. Let rise again until doubled, about 30 to 45 minutes.

6. Bake in pre-heated 375 degree oven for 40 to 45 minutes until golden brown. Remove from pans and cool on wire rack. While cooling, brush tops with melted butter.

Makes 2 large loaves.

it's a piece
of cake!

Peach Tree Carrot Cake

This is one of Hector's very favorite desserts — he justifies it by saying he's eating extra veggies!

3 cups grated carrots (approx. 4 large)
4 eggs
2 cups sugar
1½ cups vegetable oil
2 teaspoons baking soda
½ teaspoon salt
2 cups flour
1 teaspoon vanilla
1 teaspoon cinnamon
1 cup chopped pecans

1. Using an electric mixer, combine carrots, eggs, sugar, and oil. Beat well.
2. Add remaining ingredients and mix well. Pour into two greased and floured 9" round cake pans. Bake in pre-heated 350 degree oven for 45 to 50 minutes. Cool for 10 minutes in pans. Invert onto racks and cool completely.
3. Frost layers and sides with Currant Frosting.

Makes 12 servings.

Currant Frosting:
8 ounces cream cheese, softened
1 pound box powdered sugar
½ cup currants

1. Using an electric mixer or food processor, beat cream cheese until fluffy. Gradually add powdered sugar and blend well. Add currants by hand.

Note: This cake should be refrigerated because of the cream cheese frosting.

Collins Chocolate Cake

Moist, dark, chocolate, delicious - probably the VERY best chocolate cake! This recipe has been in my family for years. It's even been said that if you're not a Collins, it won't work. Go ahead and try it - the rewards are wonderful!!

4 ounces unsweetened baking chocolate
1 cup butter or margarine
1 cup brewed coffee
2 cups sugar
⅔ cup buttermilk
1 teaspoon baking soda
2 eggs
½ teaspoon cinnamon
2 teaspoons vanilla
2 cups flour

1. In a large saucepan, combine chocolate, butter or margarine, and coffee. Heat, stirring constantly, until chocolate and butter are melted. Add sugar and continue cooking over low heat until sugar is dissolved.

2. Combine buttermilk, soda, eggs, cinnamon and vanilla. Stir into chocolate mixture.

3. Stir in flour, blending well. Pour into 9" X 13" pan that has been greased and floured. Bake in a pre-heated 350 degree oven for 30 minutes or until toothpick inserted in center comes out clean. Frost with Collins Chocolate Frosting.

Serves 12.

Collins Chocolate Frosting:
½ cup butter, softened
¾ cup cocoa
3 cups powdered sugar
1 teaspoon vanilla
¼ cup brewed coffee

1. Using an electric mixer or food processor, cream butter. Add cocoa, blending well.

2. Add powdered sugar and vanilla.

3. Add coffee, a little at a time, until spreading consistency. Add more coffee, a few drops at a time if the frosting is too thick.

Williamsburg Orange-Sherry Cake

This is an elegant and beautiful cake. I like to garnish the top or sides with toasted, chopped walnuts.

1 cup golden raisins
½ cup dry sherry
¾ cup butter, room temperature
½ cup brown sugar
1 cup granulated sugar
3 eggs
1½ teaspoons vanilla
Zest of 1 orange
2½ cups flour
1½ teaspoons baking soda
½ teaspoon salt
1½ cups buttermilk
½ cup chopped walnuts or pecans

1. Soak raisins in sherry overnight.
2. Using an electric mixer, cream the butter and the brown and granulated sugars together in a large bowl. Add the eggs, one at a time, beating well after each addition. Beat in the vanilla and the orange zest.
3. Combine the flour, baking soda, and salt. Add alternately with the buttermilk, beating well after each addition. Stir in nuts and raisins with the sherry.
4. Pour the batter into three greased and floured 9" round cake pans. Bake in pre-heated 350 degree oven for 35 to 40 minutes or until toothpick inserted in center comes out clean. Cool cakes in pans for 10 minutes. Invert on wire racks and cool completely. Frost layers and sides with Cream Cheese Frosting.

Serves 12.

Cream Cheese Frosting:
¼ cup butter, room temperature
8 ounces cream cheese, room temperature
1 pound powdered sugar
2 tablespoons orange liqueur
2 tablespoons orange zest

1. Using an electric mixer, cream the butter and cream cheese. Add the powdered sugar and orange liqueur. Beat until smooth and add the zest. This frosts three layers and sides of cake.

✚

Italian Cream Cake

5 extra large eggs, separated (use 6 eggs, if necessary)
2 cups sugar, divided
1 cup butter
½ teaspoon salt
1½ teaspoons vanilla
1 teaspoon baking soda
1 cup buttermilk
2 cups flour
1 cup finely chopped walnuts or pecans
1 cup flaked coconut
Garnish: Additional coconut

1. Have all ingredients at room temperature. Using an electric mixer, beat egg whites until soft peaks form. Slowly add ½ cup sugar and beat until the consistency of meringue. Set aside.
2. Cream butter, the remaining sugar, salt and vanilla, adding egg yolks one at a time until consistency of whipped cream. Stir baking soda into buttermilk. Add this mixture alternately with flour to butter mixture, beginning and ending with flour.
3. Fold in egg white mixture, then nuts and coconut. Pour batter into three 9" cake pans which have been greased and floured. Bake in a pre-heated 325 degree oven for approximately 40 minutes. Remove from oven. Cool 5 to 10 minutes. Remove from pan and cool completely on racks.
4. Frost 3 layers and sides of cooled cake with Italian Cream Frosting. Sprinkle extra coconut on top of cake.

Serves 12.

Note: Cake should be refrigerated if not eaten the day it is made.

Italian Cream Cake Frosting:
¾ cup butter
12 ounces cream cheese
1½ teaspoons vanilla
Approximately 1½ pounds powdered sugar

1. Have all ingredients at room temperature. Using a mixer, cream together the butter, cream cheese and vanilla.
2. Gradually add powdered sugar, and beat well. Makes enough frosting for a 3-layer cake.

Raspberry Walnut Cake

The pink frosting, with toasted chopped walnuts, makes this a very pretty cake — and it is DELICIOUS! Dress it up for a party with fresh pansies and violets.

5 extra large eggs, separated (use 6 eggs if necessary)
2 cups sugar, divided
1 cup butter
½ teaspoon salt
1½ teaspoons vanilla
1 teaspoon baking soda
1 cup buttermilk
2 cups flour
1½ cups finely chopped walnuts, divided
1 cup strained raspberry preserves

1. Have all ingredients at room temperature. Using an electric mixer, beat egg whites until soft peaks form. Gradually add ½ cup sugar and beat until the consistency of meringue. Set aside.

2. Cream butter, the remaining sugar, salt and vanilla, adding egg yolks one at a time, until consistency of whipped cream. Stir baking soda into buttermilk. Add this mixture alternately with flour to butter mixture, beginning and ending with flour.

3. Fold in egg white mixture and then add 1 cup walnuts. Pour batter into three 9" cake pans which have been greased and floured. Bake in pre-heated 325 degree oven for approximately 40 minutes or until toothpick inserted in center comes out clean. Remove from oven and cool in pans for 5 to 10 minutes. Invert onto wire racks and cool completely.

4. On the first layer, spread ¼ cup preserves; then spread with a small amount of Raspberry Cream Cheese Frosting. Repeat with second layer.

5. Top with third layer. Frost top and sides with remaining cream cheese frosting. Carefully spread the remaining ½ cup preserves on only the top of the cake. Sprinkle remaining ½ cup chopped walnuts on top of preserves.

Serves 12.

Note: Cake should be refrigerated if not eaten the day it is made.

Raspberry Cream Cheese Frosting:
    ½ **cup butter**
    12 ounces cream cheese
    ¼ **cup strained raspberry preserves**
    1½ teaspoons vanilla
    Approximately 1½ pounds powdered sugar

1. Have all ingredients at room temperature. Using an electric mixer, cream together the butter, cream cheese, preserves, and vanilla.

2. Gradually add powdered sugar. Makes enough frosting for a 3 layer cake.

Fresh Apple Walnut Cake

Consider yourself blessed if you have this cake left over - it just gets better and better every day. I have even been known to have some for breakfast!

1½ cups vegetable oil
2 cups granulated sugar
3 eggs
2 cups unbleached flour
⅛ teaspoon ground cloves
1¼ teaspoons cinnamon
¼ teaspoon nutmeg
1 teaspoon baking soda
¾ teaspoon salt
1 cup whole wheat flour
1¼ cups chopped walnuts
3¼ cups grated, peeled apples (about 5 or 6 apples — we use
    Granny Smith's green apples)
3 tablespoons applejack

1. Using an electric mixer, beat oil and sugar in a large bowl until thick and opaque. Add eggs, one at a time, beating well after each addition.

2. Mix together flour, cloves, cinnamon, nutmeg, baking soda, and salt, then stir in whole wheat flour. Add to oil and egg mixture and mix until well blended.

3. Add walnuts, the grated apples, and applejack all at once and stir batter until well mixed. Pour batter into a 10" bundt cake pan which has been greased and floured. Bake in a pre-heated 325 degree oven for 1 hour and 15 minutes, or until a toothpick inserted in the center comes out clean. Let cake cool for 10 minutes and then unmold. Serve with warm Apple Cider Sauce.

Serves 16.

Apple Cider Sauce:
  ½ cup butter
  ½ cup brown sugar
  1½ cups granulated sugar
  ¾ cup applejack
  1 cup sweet cider or apple juice
  ½ cup fresh orange juice
  ½ cup evaporated milk

1. Melt butter in a saucepan and stir in both sugars. Add remaining ingredients, stir and bring to boil.

2. Reduce heat and cook for 5 minutes. Remove from heat and cool slightly. Serve warm over sliced cake, about 3 tablespoons per serving.

Lemon Yogurt Cake

1 cup butter, softened
1½ cups sugar, divided
4 eggs
1 tablespoon lemon zest
1 teaspoon vanilla
2½ cups flour
1 teaspoon baking powder
1 teaspoon baking soda
¼ teaspoon salt
1 cup plain lowfat yogurt
¾ cup sliced almonds
½ cup fresh lemon juice

1. Using an electric mixer, beat the butter in a large mixing bowl until light and fluffy. Slowly beat in 1 cup of the sugar. Add the eggs, one at a time, beating thoroughly after each addition. Beat in the lemon zest and vanilla.

2. Combine the flour, baking powder, baking soda and salt in a medium bowl. Fold ⅓ of the dry ingredients into the butter mixture and then fold in ⅓ of the yogurt. Repeat 2 more times with the remaining flour and yogurt.

3. Fold in the almonds. Spoon the batter into a 9" bundt pan which has been greased and floured. Bake in a pre-heated 350 degree oven for 1 hour, or until a toothpick inserted in the center comes out clean.

4. Meanwhile, in a small non-aluminum saucepan, heat the remaining ½ cup sugar and the lemon juice until the sugar dissolves, about 5 minutes. Slowly pour the hot lemon syrup evenly over the cake while still in the pan. Let cool completely in the pan before unmolding. May be served with fruit or sauce.

Makes 16 servings.

Ricotta and Apricot Brandy Cake

5 eggs, room temperature
2 cups sugar
1 cup ricotta cheese
1 cup butter, melted and cooled
1 tablespoon orange zest
2 teaspoons vanilla
5 tablespoons apricot brandy, divided
½ teaspoon salt
2 teaspoons baking powder
3 cups flour
½ cup apricot preserves

1. Using an electric mixer, beat eggs and sugar in a large bowl until pale yellow. Add ricotta cheese, butter, orange zest, vanilla and 2 tablespoons brandy.

2. Combine salt, baking powder and flour. Add to ricotta cheese mixture.

3. Pour ¾ of the batter into a greased and floured 10" bundt pan and put a ring of chopped apricot preserves on batter and cover with the rest of batter.

4. Bake in a pre-heated 350 degree oven for 1 hour and 15 minutes until golden, and toothpick inserted in center comes out clean. Cool in pan on rack 15 minutes. Drizzle 1 tablespoon of brandy onto bottom of cake. Invert onto rack and pour the remaining 2 tablespoons brandy over cake. Glaze with Red Currant-Apricot Glaze.

Serves 16.

Red Currant-Apricot Glaze:

½ tablespoon red currant jelly
2 tablespoons pureed apricot preserves
1 tablespoon apricot brandy

1. In a small saucepan, heat jelly and preserves until thoroughly mixed. Add brandy and mix well. Brush on warm cake.

Rich Cream Cheese Pound Cake

This cake can be served with English Lemon Sauce, with seasonal fresh fruit, or by itself with afternoon tea.

¾ cup butter
6 ounces cream cheese
1½ cups sugar
1 teaspoon vanilla
4 eggs
1¾ cups flour
½ teaspoon baking powder
¼ teaspoon salt
Powdered sugar

1. Have butter, cream cheese and eggs at room temperature. Using an electric mixer, beat butter and cream cheese until creamy. Gradually add sugar, beating at medium speed 4 to 5 minutes. Add vanilla and eggs, one at a time, beating 1 minute after each addition.

2. Combine flour, baking powder and salt. Gradually add to cream cheese mixture. Beat at low speed until blended.

3. Pour batter into greased and floured 10" bundt pan. Bake 55 minutes in a pre-heated 325 degree oven. Cool 10 minutes in pan. Remove from pan and cool completely on wire rack. Sprinkle powdered sugar on top.

Serves 10 - 12.

Orange Chocolate Teacake

When I was a little girl, I discovered how wonderful it was to eat chocolate and orange together! This cake is great just sliced, but some of our customers have been known to ask for it served in a pool of fudge sauce.

1½ cups butter, softened
1½ cups sugar, divided
2 oranges
1½ teaspoons orange liqueur
8 eggs, separated, at room temperature
2 cups flour
½ teaspoon salt
¾ cup semi-sweet chocolate chips, coarsely chopped

1. Using an electric mixer, cream butter in a large bowl. Gradually beat in 1¼ cups sugar. Zest the oranges. Squeeze them, and add enough orange juice to the zest to make ⅓ cup. Beat the orange juice, zest, and the orange liqueur into the butter mixture.

2. Add the egg yolks one at a time, beating thoroughly after each addition. Beat until the mixture is very light.

3. In a separate bowl, beat the egg whites until they form soft peaks. Add the remaining ¼ cup of sugar and beat until the whites are stiff but not dry.

4. Sift the flour and salt, ⅓ at a time, over the egg yolk mixture, folding it in after each addition.

5. Stir in ¼ of the egg whites into the butter-flour mixture, and then fold in the remaining whites. Fold in the chocolate chips. Pour the batter into a greased and floured 10" bundt pan. Bake in a pre-heated 350 degree oven for 1 hour, until a toothpick inserted in the center of the cake comes out clean. Let cool for 5 minutes before turning the cake out onto a wire rack. May be iced with a chocolate glaze.

Serves 16.

Old-Fashioned Gingerbread

This is a wonderful recipe. Try it as a pineapple upside down cake and for sure in the summer, turn it into peach upside down cake! What a hit!

1 cup butter
1 cup brown sugar
1 cup molasses
1 cup boiling water
4 large eggs
2½ cups flour
½ teaspoon salt
1½ teaspoons baking soda
1 teaspoon cinnamon
1 teaspoon ginger
1 teaspoon allspice

1. Combine butter, brown sugar and molasses in bowl. Add boiling water and stir until butter is melted. Add the eggs and beat well.

2. Combine the remaining dry ingredients and add to the egg mixture. Continue stirring until batter is smooth.

3. Pour batter into a buttered 9" X 13" pan. Bake in a pre-heated 325 degree oven for 50 to 60 minutes or until a toothpick inserted in center comes out clean.

Lemon Poppy Seed Teacake

This was one of our first Tea Room desserts - it's light and very tasty, and popular in the spring. We serve each slice with a dollop of lemon sauce, and garnish each with a mint leaf and a fresh violet. Imagine how pretty it would look on a tall crystal cake stand, surrounded by a garland of ivy, violets and pansies.

1½ cups butter, softened
1¾ cups sugar, divided
2 tablespoons lemon zest
1 tablespoon orange zest
½ cup poppy seeds
8 eggs, separated, at room temperature
2 cups flour
½ teaspoon salt
½ cup fresh lemon juice

1. Using an electric mixer, cream the butter in a large bowl. Gradually beat in 1¼ cups sugar. Beat in the lemon zest, orange zest, and the poppy seeds. Add the egg yolks one at a time, beating thoroughly after each addition. Beat until the mixture is very light.

2. In a separate bowl, beat the egg whites until they form soft peaks. Gradually add ¼ cup sugar and beat until the whites are stiff but not dry.

3. Add the flour and salt, ⅓ at a time, to the egg yolk mixture, folding it in after each addition.

4. Stir in ¼ of the egg whites into the flour-egg yolk mixture and then fold in the remaining whites. Pour into 10" bundt pan which has been greased and floured. Bake in a pre-heated 350 degree oven for about one hour, or until toothpick inserted in center of the cake comes out clean. When done, let stand for 5 minutes. Remove from pan and place on a wire rack.

5. In small non-aluminum saucepan, combine lemon juice and remaining ¼ cup sugar. Heat just until sugar is dissolved. Slowly drizzle over warm cake. Serve with English Lemon Sauce (see recipe).

Makes 16 servings.

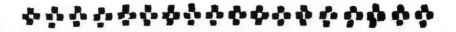

Chocolate Amaretto Cake

A real hit at our catered events! We bake two — one sits elegantly on the cake stand, and the other one is sliced and arranged on a platter nearby! It's nice served with fresh berries and Crème Fraîche.

8 ounces unsweetened baking chocolate, melted
3 cups flour
1½ teaspoons baking soda
½ teaspoon salt
6 tablespoons instant coffee granules
1 cup amaretto, divided
1½ cups butter, softened
1½ teaspoons vanilla
3 cups sugar
4 eggs

1. Grease and flour a 10" bundt cake pan. Set aside melted chocolate to cool.

2. Mix flour, soda and salt in mixing bowl. Set aside.

3. In 4 cup measuring cup, add instant coffee to a little bit of hot water. Add enough cold water to make 2¼ cups. Add ¾ cup amaretto to coffee mixture. Set aside.

4. Using an electric mixer, cream butter. Add vanilla and sugar, mixing well. Add eggs one at a time, and blend well. Add melted chocolate.

5. On low speed, alternately add dry ingredients and coffee-amaretto mixture, scraping down sides of bowl occasionally. The batter will be thin. Pour into prepared pan and rotate briskly to level.

6. Bake 1 hour and 30 minutes in a pre-heated 325 degree oven or until toothpick inserted in center comes out clean.

7. Cool in pan 15 minutes. Invert on wire rack and sprinkle with remaining ¼ cup amaretto. May be topped with chocolate glaze and a sprinkling of toasted sliced almonds.

Serves 16 - 18.

Chocolate Glaze:
  2 tablespoons butter, melted
  2 tablespoons cocoa
  ¼ cup powdered sugar
  Milk or cream

1. Combine butter and cocoa. Add powdered sugar and mix well. Gradually add milk or cream, 1 tablespoon at a time until spreading consistency. Drizzle on top of cake, allowing some to run down sides of cake.

Makes ⅓ cup.

Dobosch Torte

I was really impressed when I was first served this delicious cake in Juli Dodds' home. Not only was it good, it made a very elegant dessert! Add fresh flowers on top for a nice accent.

  1 16-ounce Sara Lee frozen pound cake
  1½ cups strained raspberry preserves
  2 cups semi-sweet chocolate chips
  1 cup sour cream
  1 teaspoon vanilla
  2 teaspoons raspberry, cherry or orange liqueur

1. Carefully slice the frozen pound cake into five or six horizontal layers. (This should be done while frozen)
2. Spread each layer with the preserves, stacking the layers evenly on top of one another.
3. In a double boiler, over hot water, melt the chocolate chips with the sour cream. Remove from heat and stir in the vanilla and liqueur.
4. Reserve ⅔ cup of the frosting. Spread the remaining warm chocolate over the top and sides of the cake. Refrigerate.
5. Just before serving, fit a pastry bag with a decorative tip, and fill with the cooled chocolate mixture. Pipe a decorative border on the top and sides of the cake.

Serves 10 - 12.

Bittersweet Chocolate Cake

This is a very rich cake, so be sure to serve thin slices. It makes a beautiful presentation when decorated with a dollop of whipped cream and a candied (or fresh) violet. While its baking, it nearly rises out of our pans. As it cools, it sinks down to a 2½ inch rich, dense torte-like cake. It's perfect for all special occasions where you have chocoholics present!

Butter
Granulated sugar
2½ cups semi-sweet chocolate chips
3 tablespoons cold water
12 eggs, separated
2 cups granulated sugar
¾ pound plus 4 tablespoons butter, softened
1 cup flour (this is the correct measurement!)
Powdered sugar

1. Butter and sugar a 10" springform pan and tap out any extra sugar.

2. Place chocolate chips in top part of a double boiler with the 3 tablespoons of cold water. Melt over simmering water, whisking until smooth. Let chocolate cool slightly.

3. Using a mixer, beat egg yolks with the 2 cups granulated sugar until thick and pale yellow, and mixture forms a ribbon when it falls from the beater.

4. Stir in warm chocolate, and the very soft butter, blending well. Fold in the flour. Mix thoroughly but gently.

5. Using a mixer (with clean beaters) beat egg whites until stiff. Stir a large spoonful of the chocolate mixture into the beaten egg whites. Mix well.

6. Pour this mixture into chocolate mixture; fold together gently, incorporating whites completely. Be very careful at this stage not to overmix.

7. Turn batter into prepared springform pan. It will come close to the top of the pan. Set on the middle rack of the oven and bake for 1 hour and 20 minutes in a pre-heated 325 degree oven, or until toothpick inserted in center comes out clean.

8. Cool on rack for 15 minutes, then remove outer rim. Allow cake to cool completely before removing bottom of pan. Refrigerate. When ready to serve, using a paper doily as a stencil, sprinkle with confectioner's sugar to make a design. Serve cold.

Makes 18 - 24 rich servings.

The Very Best Cheesecake Collection

Black Forest Cherry Cheesecake

This is our cheesecake version of the famous German Torte. It is as pretty as it is delicious. We serve it with a puff of whipped cream and Ghirardelli chocolate curls, and topped with a cherry.

Crust:
>   1¼ cups graham cracker crumbs
>   6 tablespoons melted butter
>   ½ cup cocoa (we use Ghirardelli)
>   ¼ sugar
>   ½ cup chopped pecans or almonds
>   ¼ teaspoon almond extract

1. Mix crust ingredients thoroughly and press into bottom of a well-buttered 9" to 10" springform pan. Bake in a pre-heated 325 degree oven for 15 minutes. Remove from oven and increase oven temperature to 375 degrees.

Filling:
>   24 ounces cream cheese, softened
>   1 cup sugar
>   4 eggs
>   16½-ounce can pitted bing cherries, drained and cut into halves, reserving liquid
>   ¼ cup cherry brandy
>   1 teaspoon vanilla
>   ¾ teaspoon almond extract

1. Using an electric mixer, beat cream cheese until fluffy and smooth. Add sugar and eggs, blending well after each addition.
2. Add ½ cup reserved cherry juice, brandy, vanilla and almond extract. Beat until light and creamy.
3. Pour ½ of cream cheese mixture into prepared springform pan. Bake 15 minutes at 375 degrees. Remove from oven and top with ½ of the drained cherries. Pour in remaining cream cheese mixture and top with remaining cherries. Bake 45 minutes more in the 375 degree oven. Remove from oven and cool 5 minutes. Spread with topping mixture.

Topping:
>   2 cups sour cream
>   1 tablespoon sugar
>   1 teaspoon vanilla

1. Mix topping ingredients until smooth and spread over top of baked cheesecake.

2. Return to oven and bake 5 to 8 minutes. Remove from oven and cool for several hours. Refrigerate overnight. This cheesecake is quite soft but it will firm as it cools.

Serves 14 - 16.

The Peach Tree Cheesecake

We have served this cheesecake since we opened the Tea Room and it continues to be our most popular one. It adapts well to sauces and fresh fruit. We serve it with warm praline sauce.

Crust:
1¼ cups graham cracker crumbs
¼ cup sugar
¼ cup chopped walnuts or pecans
¼ cup melted butter

1. Mix the crust ingredients thoroughly and press into the bottom of a well-buttered 9" to 10" springform pan. Bake 15 minutes in a pre-heated 325 degree oven. Remove from oven and reduce temperature to 300 degrees.

Filling:
32 ounces cream cheese, softened
1½ cups brown sugar
3 tablespoons flour
2¼ teaspoons vanilla
4 eggs
1 cup evaporated milk

1. Using an electric mixer, beat softened cream cheese with brown sugar until well blended.

2. Add flour, vanilla, and the eggs — one at a time, blending well after each.

3. Gradually add evaporated milk. Scrape down sides of bowl frequently and remix until no lumps remain. Pour into prepared pan.

4. Bake 1 hour at 300 degrees. Turn off oven and let the cake cool in oven with the door closed for several hours or overnight. Refrigerate. Can be served plain, with fresh fruit, or warm praline sauce.

Serves 14 - 16 slices.

Peach Cheesecake

Evelyn Geistweidt (our pastry lady chef in residence) created this during the height of peach season. Be sure to garnish with fresh peach slices. During peach season here in Fredericksburg, we try to eat as many peaches as we can!

Crust:
> 1½ cups graham cracker crumbs
> 6 tablespoons melted butter
> ¼ cup sugar

1. Mix the crust ingredients and press into the bottom of a well-buttered 9" to 10" springform pan. Bake 15 minutes in a pre-heated 325 degree oven. Remove from oven and reduce temperature to 300 degrees.

Filling:
> 1 cup sliced firm fresh peaches
> 32 ounces cream cheese, softened
> 1⅓ cups sugar
> 4 eggs, separated
> 1 tablespoon lemon juice
> 2 teaspoons vanilla
> 2 teaspoons almond extract
> ½ cup evaporated milk

1. Using a food processor or blender, process peaches. Set aside.
2. Using an electric mixer, beat the cream cheese with the sugar. Add the egg yolks, lemon juice, vanilla, almond extract, and evaporated milk. Mix well.
3. Add the peach purée, mixing until well blended.
4. Whip the egg whites until stiff and fold into cream cheese and peach mixture.
5. Pour into prepared springform pan. Bake at 300 degrees for 1 hour. Turn off oven and allow cheesecake to cool in oven with door closed for several hours. Refrigerate overnight. Garnish with whipped cream, mint and fresh peach slice.

Serves 14 - 16.

Last Lime Cheesecake

Evelyn and I developed this recipe and it got its name from the many improvements we made along the way. When we were satisfied with the finished product, we called it the Last Lime Cheesecake!

Crust:
1¼ cups graham cracker crumbs
¼ cup sugar
¼ cup chopped walnuts or pecans
¼ cup melted butter

1. Mix the crust ingredients thoroughly, and press into the bottom of a well buttered 9" to 10" springform pan. Bake 15 minutes in a preheated 325 degree oven. Remove from oven.

Filling:
32 ounces cream cheese, softened
1¼ cups sugar
5 eggs, separated
6 tablespoons freshly squeezed lime juice
3 tablespoons lime zest
1 cup evaporated milk
2 teaspoons vanilla

1. Using an electric mixer, beat the cream cheese with the sugar. Add the egg yolks, lime juice, zest, evaporated milk, and vanilla. Mix well.

2. Whip the egg whites until stiff and fold into cream cheese mixture.

3. Pour into prepared springform pan and bake for 1 hour at 325 degrees.

4. Remove from oven and cool for 5 minutes. Spread with topping mixture.

Topping:
2 cups sour cream
3 tablespoons sugar
1 teaspoon vanilla

1. Combine topping ingredients and spread over top of baked cheesecake.

2. Return to oven and bake 5 to 8 minutes. Remove from oven and cool for several hours. Refrigerate overnight.

Serves 14 - 16.

Lemon Blueberry Cheesecake

You will love the lemon custard topping on this cheesecake. It adds just the right amount of tartness to compliment the blueberries.

Crust:
1¼ cups graham cracker crumbs
¼ cup sugar
¼ cup chopped walnuts or pecans
¼ cup melted butter

1. Mix the crust ingredients thoroughly and press into the bottom of a well-buttered 9" to 10" springform pan. Bake 15 minutes in a preheated 325 degree oven. Remove from oven and reduce temperature to 300 degrees.

Filling:
32 ounces cream cheese, softened
1½ cups brown sugar
3 tablespoons flour
2¼ teaspoons vanilla
4 eggs
1 cup evaporated milk
1 cup frozen or fresh blueberries
⅓ cup granulated sugar
1 cup English Lemon Sauce (see recipe)

1. Using an electric mixer, beat softened cream cheese with brown sugar until well blended. Add flour, vanilla, and eggs, blending well after each addition.

2. Gradually add evaporated milk. Mix well.

3. Pour half of cream cheese mixture into prepared springform pan. Bake 15 minutes in a 300 degree oven. Remove from oven.

4. Combine blueberries with sugar. Sprinkle ½ cup sugared blueberries on top of partially baked cheesecake. Pour remaining cream cheese mixture over blueberry layer. Top with remaining blueberries. Continue baking in 300 degree oven for 45 minutes. Remove from oven.

5. Top with 1 cup English Lemon Sauce. Bake 8 to 10 minutes more. Turn off oven and let cheesecake cool in oven with door closed for several hours or overnight. Refrigerate.

Serves 14 - 16.

* Texas Pie * pasture of wooden blue

bonnets *

Jeep's boot | * pie crust stars *

* yellow rose of Texas *

Rasberry Walnut cake

Notes

Apricot Cheesecake

This is a light and fluffy cheesecake because of the beaten egg whites. When we serve it, we add a puff of whipped cream, fresh mint leaves, and a bright yellow cosmos flower. Our customers love the presentation!

Crust:
>1½ cups graham cracker crumbs
>6 tablespoons melted butter
>¼ cup sugar

1. Mix the crust ingredients and press into the bottom of a well-buttered 9" to 10" springform pan. Bake 15 minutes in a pre-heated 325 degree oven. Remove from oven and reduce temperature to 300 degrees.

Filling:
>½ cup boiling water
>1 cup dried apricots
>½ cup boiling water
>1⅓ cups sugar
>32 ounces cream cheese, softened
>6 eggs, separated
>1 tablespoon lemon juice
>1½ teaspoons lemon zest
>2 tablespoons vanilla
>1 cup evaporated milk

1. Pour boiling water over apricots. Cover with plastic wrap and let apricots soften, about 30 minutes. Drain and process the apricots in a blender with half the sugar. Cool.

2. Using an electric mixer, beat the cream cheese and add the remainder of the sugar. Add the egg yolks, lemon juice and zest, vanilla, and evaporated milk. Mix well.

3. Whip the egg whites until they are stiff and fold them into the cream cheese mixture.

4. Fold the apricot purée into the filling and pour into the prepared springform pan. Bake at 300 degrees for 1 hour. Turn off oven and allow the cheesecake to cool in oven with door closed for several hours. Refrigerate overnight.

Serves 14 - 16.

Pumpkin Cheesecake

This is a popular cheesecake for the fall season. We served it for dessert at Thanksgiving and it proved to be a hit. We are especially proud that Gourmet Magazine published our recipe in their March, 1989, issue.

Crust:
>   1¼ cups graham cracker crumbs
>   ½ cup finely chopped pecans
>   ¼ cup brown sugar
>   ¼ cup granulated sugar
>   ¼ cup butter, melted

1. Combine all ingredients and mix well. Pat mixture firmly into bottom only of a buttered 9" to 10" springform pan. Bake 15 minutes in a pre-heated 325 degree oven. Remove from oven and set aside. Reduce oven to 300 degrees.

Filling:
>   ¾ cup granulated sugar
>   1 cup canned pumpkin
>   3 eggs
>   1½ teaspoons cinnamon
>   ½ teaspoon nutmeg
>   ½ teaspoon ground ginger
>   ½ teaspoon salt
>   24 ounces cream cheese, softened
>   6 tablespoons granulated sugar
>   1 tablespoon cornstarch
>   2 tablespoons evaporated milk or whipping cream
>   ½ teaspoon vanilla

1. Mix ¾ cup sugar, pumpkin, eggs, cinnamon, nutmeg, ginger, and salt in a bowl. Set aside.

2. Using an electric mixer, beat the cream cheese and 6 tablespoons sugar until smooth.

3. Add cornstarch, evaporated milk, and vanilla, beating well after each addition.

4. Add pumpkin mixture to cream cheese mixture. Mix until no traces of white remain.

5. Pour filling mixture into prepared springform pan, and bake 1 hour at 300 degrees until sides have risen. The center will be soft.

6. Turn off oven and let cake cool with door closed for several hours or overnight. Refrigerate cheesecake. May be served with whipped

cream, a dusting of cinnamon, sugar, and a few small pieces of toffee candy, if desired. Also would be good topped with our praline sauce.

Serves 14 - 16.

Chocolate Cheesecake

We serve this cheesecake in the Tea Room with whipped cream and fresh strawberry slices. This could well be the ultimate dessert for chocolate lovers!

Crust:
> 1¼ cups graham cracker crumbs
> 6 tablespoons melted butter
> ½ cup cocoa (we use Ghirardelli)
> ¼ cup sugar
> ½ cup chopped walnuts or pecans

1. Mix crust ingredients thoroughly and press into bottom of well-buttered 9" to 10" springform pan. Bake in a pre-heated 325 degree oven for 15 minutes. Remove from oven.

Filling:
> 24 ounces cream cheese, softened
> 1 cup sugar
> 3 eggs
> 1½ cups chocolate chips, melted
> 2 tablespoons cocoa
> 1 teaspoon vanilla
> 2 cups sour cream

1. Using an electric mixer, beat cream cheese until fluffy and smooth.

2. Add sugar and beat in the eggs, one at a time.

3. Stir in melted chocolate, cocoa, and vanilla, beating well after each addition.

4. Add sour cream and continue beating until very smooth and well blended. Do not overbeat.

5. Pour into prepared springform pan and bake for 1 hour and 10 minutes at 325 degrees.

6. Turn off oven and allow the cheesecake to cool in oven with door closed for several hours. Refrigerate overnight. The cheesecake may appear to be liquid, but will firm up when chilled.

Serves 14 - 16.

Amaretto Cheesecake

This looks and tastes wonderful with sliced fresh strawberries!

Crust:
- 1¼ cups graham cracker crumbs
- 6 tablespoons melted butter
- ½ cup cocoa (we use Ghirardelli)
- ¼ cup sugar
- ½ cup chopped walnuts, pecans, or almonds
- ¼ teaspoon almond extract

1. Mix crust ingredients thoroughly and press into bottom of well-buttered 9" to 10" springform pan. Bake in a pre-heated 325 degree oven for 15 minutes. Remove from oven and increase oven temperature to 375 degrees.

Filling:
- 24 ounces cream cheese, softened
- 1 cup sugar
- 4 eggs
- ⅓ cup evaporated milk
- ¼ cup amaretto
- 1 teaspoon vanilla
- ¾ teaspoon almond extract

1. Using an electric mixer, beat cream cheese until fluffy and smooth. Add sugar and eggs. Blend well.

2. Add evaporated milk, amaretto, vanilla, and almond extract. Beat until light and creamy.

3. Pour batter into prepared springform pan, and bake 40 to 45 minutes at 375 degrees.

4. Remove from oven and cool for 5 minutes. Spread with topping mixture.

Topping:
- 2 cups sour cream
- 1 tablespoon sugar
- 1 teaspoon vanilla

1. Mix topping ingredients until smooth and spread over top of baked cheesecake.

2. Return to oven and bake 5 to 8 minutes. Remove from oven and cool for several hours. Refrigerate overnight. This cake is quite soft but will firm as it cools.

Serves 14 - 16.

Happy Endings
Just Desserts

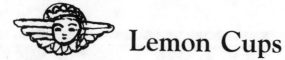

Lemon Cups

This has cake on top and a tart, lemony custard on the bottom - very delicate and light!

1 cup sugar
¼ cup flour
⅛ teaspoon salt
2 tablespoons melted butter
1½ tablespoons lemon zest
6 tablespoons fresh lemon juice, strained
3 egg yolks, beaten
1½ cups milk
3 egg whites, stiffly beaten

1. Combine sugar, flour, salt, melted butter, lemon zest, lemon juice, egg yolks, and milk. Blend well.
2. Fold in beaten egg whites.
3. Spoon into 6 to 8 lightly greased 6-ounce custard cups. Set the cups in a large pan and half fill the pan with water. Bake in a pre-heated 350 degree oven for 40 minutes. Serve slightly warm or cold.

Serves 6 - 8.

Russian Crème

This is my mother's original recipe, created after she tasted it in New York City in 1945! In the Tea Room we serve each Russian Crème with Strawberry Sauce - either fresh or cooked from frozen berries. We top each with a fresh berry and a mint sprig. We've also done this in one large mold for a buffet. It's a lovely presentation when unmolded in a pool of Strawberry Sauce and surrounded by mint.

½ cup sugar
1 cup half and half
1 tablespoon gelatin
½ cup cold water
1 cup sour cream
1 teaspoon vanilla

1. In a small saucepan, add sugar to half and half and heat until lukewarm. Stir constantly with a whisk until sugar is dissolved. Soften gelatin in water and add to warm half and half mixture.

2. Continue to stir over heat until the gelatin is dissolved. Remove from heat and refrigerate until the mixture begins to thicken.

3. Meanwhile, using an electric mixer, whip sour cream and vanilla. Gradually add thickened gelatin mixture. Continue to whip for about 1 minute until thoroughly mixed. Spray molds (approximately ⅔ cup each) with vegetable coating and pour mixture into molds.

4. Refrigerate until firm. Unmold and serve with a topping of fresh fruit, sauce, jam, etc.

Makes five ⅔-cup molds.

Flan

A elegant final touch is to pour warm brandy or rum over flan and light it just before serving.

Sauce:
1½ cups white sugar

1. Place the sugar in a heavy skillet and cook over very low heat, stirring until melted and golden brown. Watch carefully so as not to burn sugar. Pour quickly into 1½ quart mold and spread over the sides. Do this quickly, as the sugar begins to harden immediately. It will soften into a caramel sauce after it is baked.

Pudding:
**4 cups milk or half and half, or 2 cups milk and 2 cups
    evaporated milk
¾ cup sugar
⅛ teaspoon salt
6 large eggs
1 teaspoon vanilla**

1. Combine the milk, sugar, and salt in a heavy saucepan. Slowly bring to boil, and boil vigorously for 1 minute. Using an electric mixer, beat eggs. Gradually add hot mixture, beating thoroughly. Continue beating for 1 minute while mixture cools slightly. Stir in vanilla.

2. Pour mixture into prepared mold and cook in water-bath (large pan half filled with hot water) for 1½ hours in a pre-heated 300 degree oven, or until knife inserted in flan comes out clean. Cool to room temperature; chill in refrigerator. Unmold on dish with a raised edge, to hold sauce.

Serves 6.

Meringue Clouds

This is a fun recipe for entertaining! In the Tea Room, we pile in the chocolate mousse for "Mousse on a Cloud"! For Lemon Clouds, we put a dollop of English Lemon Sauce and float a strawberry slice or violet on top.

3 egg whites, room temperature
¼ teaspoon cream of tartar
¾ cup sugar

1. Using an electric mixer, beat the egg whites and the cream of tartar until foamy. Beat in the sugar, 1 tablespoon at a time. Continue beating until very stiff and glossy. Do not underbeat.
2. Cover baking sheets with heavy brown paper or cooking parchment. On the baking sheets, shape meringue into little dishes about the size of a quarter. This will make about 32 petite shells.
3. The meringue can be formed into larger single serving shells, about ⅓ cup of meringue each.
4. Bake large shells in pre-heated 225 degree oven for 90 minutes. Bake mini-shells for 45 minutes. Turn off oven. Leave in oven for at least 1 hour with door closed. (Best if left in over-night.) Remove from oven and finish cooling away from draft. Store in an airtight container.
5. The shells can be filled with the following: Cream Cheese Filling (see recipe), Chocolate Mousse (see recipe), ice cream, or English Lemon Sauce (see recipe).

Note: It is important that the shells be completely baked and dried out so that they are not sticky or chewy. If the humidity is high, they can be re-crisped in a 225 degree oven.

Cream Cheese Filling

1 cup whipping cream
3 ounces cream cheese, softened
½ cup sugar
½ teaspoon vanilla

1. Using an electric mixer, beat cream until stiff in a chilled bowl. Set aside.
2. Again using an electric mixer, blend cream cheese, sugar, and vanilla. Gently fold whipped cream into cream cheese mixture. Spoon into prepared meringue shells. Top with fresh fruit, if desired.

 # Fruit Crêpes

Crêpes (see recipe)
Cream filling (see recipe)
Sliced, sugared fruit

1. To assemble, place 1 Crêpe in large individual serving bowl. Place approximately ¼ cup cream filling along center of Crêpe. Top filling with about ¼ cup sliced fruit.

2. Gently fold Crêpe and flip over, seam side down, in bowl. Top with about ½ cup sliced fruit with juice.

3. Place dollop of cream filling in center of Crêpe and top with fresh mint and fresh flowers, if available.

Crêpes

2 eggs
2 tablespoons butter, melted
1⅓ cups milk
1 cup flour
½ teaspoon salt
1 tablespoon sugar

1. Place ingredients in blender in order given. Blend on high speed for 30 seconds. Scrape sides of blender and blend again about 20 seconds more.

2. The batter may be refrigerated at this time or used immediately. For each Crêpe, put 2 to 3 tablespoons batter into medium warm, slightly greased 6" to 7" skillet. Tilt to spread batter evenly to make thin Crêpe. When Crêpe is light brown, turn and cook on second side.

Makes 12 - 16 Crêpes.

Cream Filling for Fruit Crêpes

This is the filling we use for our peach or strawberry Crêpes. They're another very popular dessert. Remember to try the Crêpes with Fredericksburg peaches!

16 ounces cream cheese, softened
⅓ cup sugar
1 teaspoon almond extract
2 cups sour cream

1. Using a food processor or electric mixer, blend cream cheese with sugar and almond extract.
2. Mix in sour cream, blending well. Serve in Crêpes with fresh fruit.

Makes 4½ cups filling.

Crème Fraîche

This makes a wonderful topping for fruit desserts — fresh and light!

2 cups whipping cream
2 tablespoons buttermilk

1. Combine the ingredients and allow to set at room temperature for 8 to 10 hours or until thickened. Stir and refrigerate.

Makes 2 cups.

Shortcake Biscuits

These are the biscuits we use for fruit shortcakes. Split the biscuits in half, put fresh fruit inside the two layers and on top. Finish with a dollop of sweetened whipped cream, or Crème Fraîche.

2 cups flour
¼ cup sugar
3 teaspoons baking powder
½ teaspoon salt
½ cup butter, chilled
1 egg, beaten
⅔ cup evaporated milk, or half and half
Melted butter
Sugar

1. Combine dry ingredients. Using a fork or pastry cutter, cut butter into dry ingredients until a coarse texture.

2. Combine egg and milk, and add to flour mixture. Turn mixture onto lightly floured board and knead briefly. Roll to ½" thick and cut with a biscuit cutter. (We use a heart biscuit cutter in the Tea Room.)

3. Bake on an ungreased cookie sheet in a pre-heated 425 degree oven for 10 minutes. While still hot, brush with butter and sprinkle tops with sugar.

Makes 8 biscuits.

Peach Crisp

One more great way to eat Fredericksburg peaches! It's great served warm with a scoop of ice cream!

Filling:
    9 cups peeled and sliced fresh peaches
    2 teaspoons lemon juice
    ½ teaspoon almond extract

1. Toss peaches with lemon juice and almond extract. Place in buttered 9" X 13" baking dish.

Topping:
    1 cup brown sugar
    ¾ cup whole wheat flour
    3 cups quick oats
    1½ cups chopped pecans
    ¾ cup coconut
    1 cup melted butter
    1 teaspoon almond extract
    1 teaspoon nutmeg, optional

1. Combine sugar, flour, oats, pecans, and coconut. Stir in melted butter and almond extract.
2. Spread evenly over peach filling. If desired, sprinkle with nutmeg. Bake in a pre-heated 350 degree oven for 45 to 60 minutes until top is golden and the filling is bubbly around edges.

Serves 12.

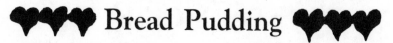

Bread Pudding

*Sometimes we make this with day-old croissants and bits of leftover cake.
It's a no fail recipe - crusty on top and moist and tender inside. Serve warm
with Custard Sauce.*

**10 to 15 1" slices of day old French bread (preferably
    homemade)**
½ cup butter, room temperature
8 eggs, beaten
1 cup granulated sugar
8 cups milk
2 tablespoons vanilla
Brown sugar
Nutmeg

1. Lightly spread top surface of bread slices with butter. Layer in
buttered 11" X 13" baking dish.

2. Combine eggs, sugar, milk, and vanilla. Mix together with a
whisk. This step can also be done in the blender.

3. Pour mixture over layered bread. The bread may not absorb all
the liquid. Save the extra egg-milk mixture. Refrigerate for 4 hours or
overnight. Add the reserved liquid until all is absorbed.

4. Sprinkle bread pudding generously with brown sugar and nutmeg. Bake in a pre-heated 325 to 350 degree oven for 1 hour until
pudding is puffed and golden, and knife inserted in center comes out
clean. Serve warm or at room temperature with Custard Sauce.

Serves 15.

Custard Sauce:
4 cups milk
4 eggs
¾ cup sugar
1 tablespoon flour
2 teaspoons vanilla

1. Heat milk to scalding in heavy saucepan.

2. Using a whisk, beat eggs with sugar and flour. Pour small amount
of hot milk into egg mixture, stirring well. Gradually add egg mixture to
remaining hot milk.

3. Cook mixture over medium heat, stirring constantly, until custard coats metal spoon. Remove from heat and add vanilla. Serve warm or cold.

Makes 5 cups.

Note: If the custard should curdle while cooking, try blending mixture in blender.

Chocolate Mousse

If you like chocolate, you'll love this! I like to serve it using an ice cream scoop. I also think it would be worth the little extra effort to pile it in a baked pie crust and circle the edges with large strawberries, mint leaves and plenty of whipped cream.

2¼ cups semi-sweet chocolate chips
⅓ cup strong brewed coffee
2 tablespoons orange liqueur (or raspberry liqueur or brandy)
2 egg yolks
½ teaspoon vanilla
4 egg whites
Pinch of salt
1 cup heavy cream, chilled
2 tablespoons sugar

1. Combine chocolate chips and coffee in a heavy saucepan. Cook over low heat stirring constantly until chips are melted. Stir in liqueur or brandy. Remove from heat and cool to room temperature.

2. Using a whisk, add egg yolks one at a time to chocolate mixture, beating thoroughly after each addition. Add vanilla.

3. Beat egg whites with salt until stiff. In another bowl, beat the heavy cream until thickened. Gradually add the sugar, beating until stiff.

4. Gently fold egg whites into the whipped cream. Stir about ⅓ of the egg white - cream mixture into the chocolate mixture. Add remaining egg white and cream mixture. Blend thoroughly but gently. Pour into individual serving dishes or one large serving bowl. Refrigerate 2 hours or overnight. Garnish with additional whipped cream and a whole strawberry or raspberry on each serving.

Serves 8.

Notes

Loving
Celebrations
♡
pastRies
and
pies

Cynthia's Basic Pie and Pastry Crust

I fondly titled this recipe "Dana's Pie Crust" in my personal cookbook. We attended cooking school together and I lost my copy. I'm grateful to her for carefully protecting this great recipe!

1½ cups unsifted unbleached flour
½ teaspoon salt
2 tablespoons Crisco shortening
6 tablespoons CHILLED butter (not margarine)
5 tablespoons ICED water

1. Mix flour and salt in bowl. Cut in Crisco and butter with a pastry blender until crumbly.

2. Add ICED water, a little at a time, mixing with a fork until well blended. Place dough into plastic bag and gently press dough together into flat disk. Refrigerate dough for 30 to 60 minutes. This allows the gluten to develop in the dough.

3. Carefully roll dough on floured board; lift into 9" to 10" pie plate, trimming dough and rolling edges under to form rim. Flute the edge. It is important not to overwork your pastry at this point; if you handle it gently, your result will be a flaky and tender crust.

4. Put a layer of foil over dough, and fill to the top with either pie weights or dry pinto beans. This prevents crust from puffing up and shrinking.

For PARTIALLY baked pie crust: Bake in a pre-heated 400 degree oven for 12 minutes. Carefully remove foil and beans. Prick crust bottom with fork several times, and bake 5 to 10 minutes more until completely dry.

For COMPLETELY baked pie crust: Bake in a pre-heated 400 degree oven for 12 minutes. Carefully remove foil and beans. Prick crust bottom with fork several times, and bake 10 to 15 minutes more until completely dry and golden in color.

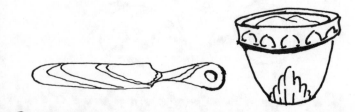

Brooke's Pie Crust

This is my friend Brooke's, fool-proof recipe for a flaky pie shell.

3 cups sifted flour
1 teaspoon salt
1 cup Crisco shortening
1 beaten egg, plus enough iced water to make ½ cup

1. Mix flour and salt. Cut in shortening with a pastry blender until consistency of coarse corn meal.

2. Add egg and water mixture and mix well with a fork. Form into a ball.

3. Divide dough in half. On lightly floured surface, roll dough and gently lift into 2 9" pie plates. Turn under edge and flute. The shells are now ready for filling.

Makes 2 shells.

Linda's Turnover Pastry

This pastry can be filled with preserves or fillings made from dried fruit. It's a fail-proof recipe. Try it!

7 cups unbleached flour
½ teaspoon salt
2 tablespoons sugar
½ teaspoon cinnamon
2½ cups Crisco shortening
1 12-ounce beer, room temperature

1. Combine flour, salt, sugar and cinnamon. Cut in shortening with a pastry cutter or use a food processor.

2. Stir in beer, mixing well. Refrigerate dough for at least 30 minutes or overnight.

3. Roll dough ⅛" thick on floured board. Cut rounds of dough about 5 to 6 inches in diameter. Place about 2 tablespoons filling in each.

4. Fold dough over. Moisten edges, seal and crimp edges. Sprinkle with sugar if desired. Bake on ungreased cookie sheet in a pre-heated 375 degree oven for 15 minutes or until golden. Remove to rack to cool. These may also be glazed after baking.

Makes approximately 40 turnovers.

Ginger Pear Pie

Bake this in the fall and celebrate "Pear Season"! Slice the pears very thin and swirl them in concentric circles.

1 unbaked 9" pie shell
3 large pears
2 eggs, beaten
⅓ cup sugar
¼ teaspoon salt
¼ teaspoon ground ginger
Pinch of nutmeg
½ teaspoon lemon zest
¼ teaspoon vanilla
¼ teaspoon almond extract
1 cup sour cream

1. Peel the pears and cut them into bite size pieces.
2. Combine the eggs with the sugar, salt, ginger, nutmeg, lemon zest, vanilla, almond extract, and sour cream. Pour half of this mixture into pie shell, and arrange the pears on top.
3. Pour the remaining mixture over the pears.

Brown Sugar Topping:
¼ cup flour
3 tablespoons brown sugar
Pinch of nutmeg
2 tablespoons butter, chilled

1. Combine the flour, brown sugar and nutmeg. Cut in the butter until the mixture resembles crumbs. Sprinkle on top of pear filling.
2. Bake in a pre-heated 350 degree oven until the filling is set and the top is golden brown, approximately 1 hour.

Gammy's Peach Pie

My grandmother's recipe - very easy, light and delicious!

1 unbaked 9" pie shell
3 cups peeled and sliced fresh peaches (preferably grown in
   Fredericksburg, of course)
2 well-beaten eggs
½ cup sugar
2 teaspoons cornstarch
½ cup evaporated milk
1 teaspoon almond extract

1. Fill pie shell with peaches.
2. Combine the well-beaten eggs, sugar, cornstarch, milk, and almond extract. Mix well and pour over peaches. Do not stir.
3. Bake 15 minutes in a pre-heated 400 degree oven. Reduce oven temperature to 350 degrees and continue baking for 50 to 60 minutes until filling is firm.

Old-Fashioned Double-Crust Apple Pie

Pastry for double crust 9" pie
8 to 9 tart apples, peeled, cored, and sliced
Zest of 1 lemon
Juice of 1 lemon
½ cup sugar
1 teaspoon cinnamon
3 tablespoons butter, cut into small pieces

1. Fill pastry-lined pie shell with sliced apples. Mound them up high.
2. Sprinkle with lemon zest and juice, sugar and cinnamon. Dot with butter.
3. Cover with second pastry top, making vents, sealing and crimping rim. Bake in a pre-heated 350 degree oven for 60 to 70 minutes, or until crust is golden brown. Cool before serving.

Sour Cream Apple Pie

Crust:

   2½ cups flour
   5 tablespoons granulated sugar
   ¾ teaspoon salt
   ¾ teaspoon ground cinnamon
   6 tablespoons butter, chilled
   6 tablespoons shortening, chilled
   6 to 8 tablespoons apple cider or juice, chilled

1. Sift flour, sugar, salt, and cinnamon into a bowl. Cut in butter and shortening with a fork or pastry cutter until mixture resembles rolled oats.

2. Moisten with 6 tablespoons cider, tossing ingredients lightly with a fork. Add up to 2 tablespoons more, if necessary. Place dough in a plastic bag and gently press dough together into a flat disk. Seal bag. Refrigerate for at least 30 minutes.

3. Cut off ⅓ of the dough and return it to the refrigerator. Roll out the other ⅔'s between 2 sheets of wax paper. Line a 9" pie pan with the dough. Trim overhang and crimp decoratively.

Filling:

   6 to 7 tart Granny Smith apples
   ⅔ cup sour cream
   ⅓ cup granulated sugar
   1 egg, lightly beaten
   ¼ teaspoon salt
   1 teaspoon vanilla
   3 tablespoons flour

1. Peel, core and thinly slice apples; whisk together sour cream, sugar, egg, salt, vanilla and flour in a large bowl. Add apples to mixture and toss well to coat. Spoon apples into pastry.

Topping:

   3 tablespoons brown sugar
   3 tablespoons granulated sugar
   1 teaspoon cinnamon
   1 cup chopped walnuts

1. Mix sugars, cinnamon and walnuts together. Sprinkle evenly over apple filling.

2. Roll out remaining pastry between sheets of wax paper to form a 10" circle. Cut in ½" strips, and arrange lattice-fashion over apples. Trim ends of strips and crimp edge of crust.

3. Bake in a pre-heated 350 degree oven for 55 to 65 minutes. If crust browns too quickly, cover loosely with foil. Pie is done when juices are bubbly and apples are tender. Serve warm or cool. Garnish with whipped cream or vanilla ice cream.

Aunt Jo's Rum Pie

This is a real whopper of a dessert! Try it with a layer of sliced bananas in the filling.

1 fully baked 9" Brooke's Pie Crust (see recipe)
2 tablespoons unflavored gelatin
¾ cup cold water
6 egg yolks
1 cup sugar
⅓ to ½ cup rum
2 cups heavy cream
Pinch of salt
Grated semi-sweet chocolate

1. Sprinkle gelatin in cold water. Heat to dissolve gelatin and set aside to cool.

2. Using an electric mixer, beat egg yolks until thick. Add sugar and beat well.

3. Add dissolved gelatin and rum to egg mixture.

4. Whip cream with salt until stiff. Fold cream into egg-rum mixture. Pour into baked pie crust. Sprinkle with chocolate. Chill thoroughly until firm.

Serves 10 - 12.

Brooke's Pecan Pie

Our customers really like this pie! The addition of lemon juice keeps it from being "just too sweet".

1 unbaked 9" Brooke's Pie Crust (see recipe)
½ cup butter (not margarine)
1 cup sugar
½ teaspoon salt
1 teaspoon vanilla
1 cup light corn syrup
3 eggs, beaten
2 teaspoons fresh lemon juice
1 cup pecans, halves or pieces

1. In saucepan, brown butter until golden. Watch carefully so as not to burn. Cool.
2. Add sugar, salt, vanilla, syrup and beaten eggs, mixing well. Add lemon juice and pecans.
3. Pour into unbaked pie shell, and bake in a pre-heated 425 degree oven for 10 minutes. Reduce to 325 degrees and bake for additional 55 minutes, or until center is firm. Cool on rack.

Aunt Marion's Pecan Pie

When I was growing up, no family gathering was complete without this dessert. It's a great recipe. If you have chocolate lovers in your family, add one cup of Ghirardelli chocolate chips. Then everyone will be happy!

1 unbaked 9" pie shell
1 cup light corn syrup
3 eggs, beaten
½ teaspoon salt
1 cup sugar
2 tablespoons salad oil
1 cup chopped pecans

1. Combine corn syrup, eggs, salt, sugar, and oil. Mix well. Stir in pecans.
2. Pour into unbaked 9" pie shell. Bake in a pre-heated 400 degree oven for 15 minutes. Reduce to 350 degrees for 30 to 40 minutes, or until knife inserted in center comes out clean.

Texas Pie

This is another of Aunt Jo's recipes - lots of sugar, but it's really good! We cut stars out of the extra pastry trimming for a Texas-style garnish on top of each slice!

1 unbaked 9" pie shell
3 cups sugar
½ cup flour
3 eggs, beaten
1½ cups milk
½ cup butter (not margarine)

1. Combine sugar and flour. Add beaten eggs.

2. In saucepan, heat milk and butter over low heat until butter is melted. Slowly add butter-milk mixture to the sugar-egg mixture, blending well with whisk.

3. Pour into unbaked pie shell, and bake in a pre-heated 350 degree oven for approximately 1 hour, or until knife inserted in center comes out clean. Cool and serve each slice garnished with whipped cream and a pastry star.

Coconut Buttermilk Pie

Our kitchen supervisor, Lydia, didn't know how much she liked to cook until she came to work at The Peach Tree. This is the delicious pie she makes at home for her family and friends. Sometimes, she brings one to share with all of us in the breakroom!

1 unbaked 9" pie shell
½ cup butter or margarine, softened
2 cups sugar
⅓ cup flour
3 eggs, well beaten
1 cup buttermilk
2 teaspoons vanilla
½ teaspoon nutmeg
1½ to 2 cups flaked coconut

1. Using an electric mixer, cream butter or margarine and sugar. Add flour and eggs, mixing well.

2. Stir in buttermilk, vanilla, nutmeg and coconut.

3. Pour into unbaked pastry shell. Bake in a pre-heated 350 degree oven for 1 hour and 20 minutes or until center is firm. Cool completely on rack before serving.

Ice Cream Pie

This is the same recipe that my Aunt Jo created for her New York City restaurant many years ago. I first tasted it when I was eight years old. It was filled with rum raisin ice cream. We fix it daily in our Tea Room now and at Christmastime, we use peppermint or pistachio ice cream to make it more festive!

7 tablespoons melted butter
¼ cup brown sugar
2 ounces unsweetened baking chocolate
½ cup semi-sweet chocolate chips
3 cups corn flakes (we use Post Toasties)
⅓ cup finely chopped walnuts or pecans, optional
1½ quarts ice cream (we use coffee or vanilla flavors)

1. In medium saucepan, melt butter, brown sugar, unsweetened chocolate and chocolate chips over low heat. Stir constantly until thoroughly mixed and sugar is dissolved.

2. In large bowl, place corn flakes and nuts. Pour warm chocolate mixture over the corn flakes, gently stirring until flakes are THOROUGHLY coated.

3. Spray 9" pie plate with vegetable coating. Gently press coated flakes evenly into pie plate. Place in freezer until firm.

4. Fill frozen chocolate shell with slightly softened ice cream. Freeze until firm. Top with Fudge Sauce, Praline Sauce, berries, or sliced fruit.

Makes 6 - 8 servings.

Baklava

I discovered this wonderful, rich dessert when my family attended the World's Fair in New York City. I enjoyed it so much that my Aunt Mella, who lived there, would mail a box of it to me on every birthday!

Pastry:
    4 cups finely chopped walnuts or pecans
    ½ cup sugar
    1 teaspoon cinnamon
    ½ teaspoon nutmeg
    1 cup butter, melted
    ½ pound frozen filo leaves, thawed

1. Combine the walnuts, sugar, cinnamon, and nutmeg in a bowl and set aside. Brush a 9" X 13" glass baking dish with melted butter.

2. Place 10 filo leaves in the dish, brushing each of them with the melted butter. Spread half of the nut mixture on the leaves. Cover with 3 more leaves, each brushed with butter. Spread on the remaining nut mixture. Place the remaining leaves, each brushed with melted butter, on top.

3. Cut the baklava into squares or diamonds before baking. Bake in a pre-heated 375 degree oven for 45 minutes, or until the pastry is light brown. Remove from oven and allow to cool. Pour cooled syrup over pastry. Allow baklava to absorb syrup for at least 4 hours or overnight.

Makes 24 very rich servings.

Syrup:
    1¼ cups sugar
    1¼ cups water
    ½ cup honey
    ½ teaspoon cinnamon
    2 to 3 cloves
    1½ teaspoons lemon juice

1. Combine all syrup ingredients in a saucepan. Bring to a boil, and simmer for 10 minutes. Remove cloves and allow to cool.

Apple Strudel Baklava

2 cups coarsely chopped, pared apples
2 cups toasted and chopped almonds or walnuts, or a mixture
   of both
⅔ cup sugar
¼ cup golden raisins
1 teaspoon lemon zest
3 tablespoons lemon juice
2 teaspoons cinnamon
½ pound frozen filo leaves, thawed
1 cup butter, melted

1. Combine the apples, nuts, sugar, raisins, lemon zest and juice and cinnamon in a bowl and set aside. Brush a 9" X 13" glass baking dish with butter.

2. Place 6 filo leaves in dish, brushing each with the melted butter. Spread ½ of the apple-nut mixture on the leaves. Layer 4 more leaves brushing each with butter. Spread on remaining apple mixture and top with 6 leaves, each brushed with butter.

3. Cut baklava into squares or diamonds before baking. Bake in a pre-heated 350 degree oven for 45 minutes, or until the pastry is golden. Remove from oven, allow to cool, and pour cooled syrup over it. As the baklava sets, the syrup is absorbed.

Makes 18 rich servings.

Syrup:
   1¼ cups sugar
   1¼ cups water
   ½ cup honey
   ½ teaspoon cinnamon
   2 to 3 cloves
   1 tablespoon lemon juice

1. Combine all syrup ingredients in a saucepan. Bring to a boil, reduce heat, and simmer for 10 minutes. Remove cloves and allow to cool.

Eccles Cakes

Early in their marriage, my good friends Sally and Ottis Layne, began the tradition of afternoon tea - time out in the midst of a busy day for catching up with one another. This recipe is one of the many nice things that has grown out of their tradition!

Pastry:
    6 tablespoons unsalted butter, chilled and cut into small bits
    2 tablespoons Crisco shortening, chilled and cut into small bits
    1½ cups flour
    ¼ teaspoon salt
    2 teaspoons sugar
    3 to 4 tablespoons ICED water

1. Using a pastry blender, combine butter, Crisco, flour, salt and sugar. Mix until the mixture resembles coarse meal, but not until it becomes oily.

2. Add 3 tablespoons ICED water all at once, stirring with a fork. Gently form dough into a ball. Add up to 1 tablespoon water if the dough crumbles. Form dough into flat disk and place in plastic bag. Refrigerate for at least 1 hour.

Filling:
    3 tablespoons honey
    2 teaspoons orange liqueur
    2 teaspoons orange juice (you may use all orange juice rather
        than liqueur)
    ¼ teaspoon cinnamon
    ¼ teaspoon nutmeg
    ¼ teaspoon allspice
    ¼ teaspoon ginger
    ¾ cup currants
    ¾ cup chopped pecans
    4 tablespoons melted butter

1. Combine all filling ingredients except butter, mixing thoroughly. Add butter and mix well.

2. Allow mixture to stand 30 minutes or overnight in refrigerator.

3. On lightly floured board, roll pastry ¼" thick. Cut out 3" circles and roll each to ⅛" thick. Place heaping tablespoon of currant-nut filling in the center of each circle. Bring up the outside edges to the center and press down. Roll with rolling pin into flat rounds. The currants will be visible below the surface when the cakes are turned over.

4. Bake cakes on ungreased cookie sheet in a pre-heated 475 degree oven for 15 minutes or until golden brown. Cool on wire rack.

Makes 8.

Caramel Sauce

This keeps well in a covered jar in the refrigerator for up to 4 months. But I bet it won't last that long - it's delicious!

1 cup light brown sugar
½ cup butter (not margarine), divided
½ cup light corn syrup
2 tablespoons heavy cream
½ teaspoon vanilla
⅛ teaspoon salt

1. In a small heavy, non-aluminum saucepan, combine brown sugar and ¼ cup butter. Bring to boil over moderate heat. Whisk in the corn syrup, cream, vanilla and salt.

2. Reduce the heat to moderately low, and boil gently for about 3 minutes, stirring constantly.

3. Immediately remove from heat and whisk in the remaining ¼ cup butter. Serve warm or at room temperature. Makes about 1½ cups.

Strawberry Sauce

Our Russian Crèmes get their sparkle from this sauce! It keeps well in the
refrigerator and is wonderful to have on hand to add pizazz to your desserts.

3 10-ounce packages frozen sliced strawberries in syrup
1 cup sugar
4½ teaspoons lemon juice

1. Thaw strawberries. Combine all ingredients and purée in blender
or food processor until thick.
2. Place in non-aluminum saucepan. Bring to boil and cook over
low heat for 10 minutes until bright red in color and thickened. Stir
occasionally to prevent scorching.
3. Remove from heat and allow to cool. Refrigerate.

Makes 3½ cups.

Fudge Sauce Delight

This is the very rich fudge sauce we use on Brownie Delights and ice
cream pies. Also great as a fondue for fresh fruit.

8 squares (8 ounces) unsweetened baking chocolate (we use
  Ghirardelli chocolate)
1½ cups water
2 cups sugar
½ teaspoon salt
¼ cup butter
1 teaspoon vanilla

1. In medium saucepan, combine chocolate and water. Cook over
low heat, stirring constantly until chocolate is melted and mixture is
smooth.
2. Add sugar and salt. Cook and stir about 5 minutes, or until sugar
is dissolved and mixture is slightly thickened.
3. Add butter and stir until melted. Remove from heat and add
vanilla.

Makes about 1 quart.

Note: Store in refrigerator when cool. It will thicken when cold but
easily softens in microwave.

Picnics-To-Go: ham & cheese croissant, fruit, and Leah's Cookie.

Notes

For Happy Birthdays - the famous Collins Chocolate Cake

Praline Sauce

We use this dark, rich sauce to top our cheesecake and ice cream pie in the Tea Room. It continues to be a favorite treat.

1 cup light brown sugar
2½ tablespoons cornstarch
1½ cups water
2 tablespoons butter or margarine
½ cup chopped pecans

1. In small saucepan, combine brown sugar and cornstarch. Add water and cook, stirring constantly over medium heat until thick and bubbly, about 5 minutes.
    2. Add butter, stirring until melted. Stir in pecans.

Makes about 2 cups.

Peach Tree Lemon Sauce

This is a wonderfully tart lemon sauce that we use on our Lemon Clouds and Poppy Seed Teacake. It's also great on angel food cake and pound cake!!

½ cup butter (not margarine)
4 eggs
2 cups sugar
½ cup plus 2 tablespoons fresh lemon juice, strained
1 tablespoon cornstarch
1 tablespoon lemon zest

1. Melt butter in non-aluminum saucepan on low heat.
    2. Using a blender or food processor, blend eggs, sugar, lemon juice and cornstarch. Add to melted butter and cook on low heat, stirring constantly. Cook until mixture is thick and bubbly, about 8 minutes.
    3. Remove from heat and add lemon zest. Serve warm or cold.

Makes about 2 cups. Keeps forever.

Notes

A cookie in hand is worth 2 in the jar

Leah's Cookies

Our son, Carlos, loves chocolate chip cookies. His good friend in Florida sent him this great recipe that we now use. For the Tea Room, we use ¼ cup cookie dough to make a larger cookie. This recipe can easily be cut in half.

5 cups quick oats
2 cups butter, softened
2 cups granulated sugar
2 cups brown sugar
4 eggs
2 teaspoons vanilla
4 cups flour
2 teaspoons baking powder
2 teaspoons baking soda
1 teaspoon salt
4½ cups semi-sweet chocolate chips
1 8-ounce milk chocolate Hershey bar, cut into ½" squares
3 cups chopped pecans or walnuts

1. In food processor or blender, process oats briefly, and set aside.
2. Using an electric mixer, cream butter and both sugars. Add eggs and vanilla and mix well.
3. Combine flour, blended oats, baking powder, baking soda, and salt. Add to butter-egg mixture, blending well.
4. Stir in chips, candy and nuts.
5. Roll into balls and place 2" apart on a cookie sheet.
6. Bake in a pre-heated 375 degree oven for 6 to 10 minutes.

Yields approximately 112 cookies.

Cowboy Cookies

*We make these TEXAS size by using ¼ cup of dough for each cookie!
It's an impressive size and our customers love them.*

½ cup butter, softened
½ teaspoon vanilla
½ cup granulated sugar
½ cup packed brown sugar
1 egg
1 cup flour
½ teaspoon baking soda
¼ teaspoon baking powder
¼ teaspoon salt
1 cup quick oats
½ cup semi-sweet chocolate chips
½ cup chopped walnuts or pecans

1. Using an electric mixer, cream the butter, adding the vanilla and both sugars and mix well.

2. Add egg and beat well.

3. Combine the flour, baking soda, baking powder and salt in a separate bowl. On low speed, gradually add the dry ingredients to the sugar mixture, and continue mixing.

4. Stir in the quick oats and the chocolate chips and nuts. The dough will be stiff.

5. Place 1 tablespoon dough about 2" apart on a greased cookie sheet, and bake 12 to 15 minutes in a pre-heated 350 degree oven.

Yields approximately 36 small cookies.

Sally's Shortbread Cookies

This is an easy recipe for baking shortbread in decorative molds. The dough can also be patted out to ½" thickness, baked, and then cut into shapes.

1 pound butter, softened
1 cup sugar
5 to 6 cups flour
1 tablespoon flavoring - lemon extract, almond extract, or
    vanilla extract
Granulated sugar

1. Using an electric mixer, cream butter and 1 cup sugar. Gradually add 5 cups flour, 1 cup at a time. Add up to 1 cup more flour, as necessary if the dough appears moist.

2. Press into 13" X 9" X 2" pan. Bake in a pre-heated 350 degree oven for 10 minutes. Remove from oven and press down the dough with the back of a fork. Return to oven and continue baking for 20 to 25 minutes, or until edges are lightly browned.

3. Remove the pan from oven to wire rack. Sprinkle with sugar and cut into squares while still hot. Cool completely.

Makes 48 squares.

Fruit Drop Cookies

These make a great cookie for Christmas giving! I like to bake these in mini-muffin tins with pretty Christmas paper liners, then glaze the tops and add a candied cherry!

½ **pound candied cherries, cut up**
½ **pound candied pineapple, cut up**
1 **pound raisins**
6 **cups pecans, broken into large chunks**
½ **cup bourbon**
½ **cup butter, softened**
1½ **cups brown sugar**
4 **eggs, beaten**
1 **tablespoon milk**
3 **cups flour**
3 **teaspoons baking soda**
1 **teaspoon allspice**

1. Soak cherries, pineapple, raisins and pecans in bourbon overnight.

2. Using an electric mixer, cream butter and brown sugar. Add eggs and milk. Mix thoroughly.

3. Combine flour, soda and allspice. Gradually add to creamed mixture. Stir in fruit and pecan mixture.

4. Drop by spoonfuls on greased cookie sheet, and bake in preheated 325 to 350 degree oven for 12 minutes. These can be iced with a thin powdered sugar and cream glaze.

Makes approximately 130 cookies.

Mincemeat Pinwheel Cookies

This is a delightful cookie to have on hand for Christmas parties and gifts!

1 cup butter, softened
2 cups light brown sugar
2 eggs
2 teaspoons almond extract
4 cups flour
2 teaspoons baking powder
½ teaspoon salt

1. Using an electric mixer, cream butter and sugar well.
2. Add eggs and almond extract. Beat until smooth and creamy.
3. Combine the flour, baking powder, and salt. Add to creamed mixture, blending well.
4. Divide dough in 2 parts. Cover and chill at least 1 hour.

Filling:

2 9-ounce boxes mincemeat
¼ cup warm water
¼ cup honey
2 eggs, beaten
2 teaspoons almond extract
1 cup walnuts or pecans, finely chopped

1. Combine all filling ingredients, mixing well.
2. On floured board, roll dough ¼" thick into a 16" x 6" rectangle.
3. Spread half the filling over dough. Roll as for a jelly roll. Repeat with second portion of dough and filling. Cover with plastic wrap and chill overnight.
4. Slice rolls into ⅛" slices, and place on greased cookie sheet.
5. Bake at 375 degrees for 20 minutes. Remove at once to wire rack to cool.

Makes 72 cookies.

Sadie's Ginger Cookies

When I was a little girl, I would go up to Michigan to visit my Aunt Jo. She had a friend named Sadie who worked for a family in Birmingham, and she baked these cookies daily. She was nice enough to give me the recipe to bring back to Texas, and I've kept it since then. Try them and you'll know why.

¾ cup shortening
1 cup sugar
2 eggs
5 tablespoons molasses
2 teaspoons baking soda
1 teaspoon ground ginger
1 teaspoon ground cinnamon
1 teaspoon ground cloves
1 teaspoon ground nutmeg
2½ cups flour
½ teaspoon salt

1. Using an electric mixer, cream shortening and sugar. Add eggs and molasses, mixing thoroughly.

2. Combine the remaining dry ingredients. Gradually add to creamed mixture, blending well.

3. Drop by tablespoons on greased cookie sheet. With a drinking glass that is well-buttered and dipped in sugar, flatten each cookie.

4. Bake in a pre-heated 350 degree oven for 12 minutes. Cool slightly before removing from pan. Cool on wire racks.

Yields approximately 36 3" cookies.

Lydia's Molasses Oatmeal Cookies

½ cup margarine or butter
½ cup sugar
½ cup molasses
2 eggs
1¼ cups flour
¾ teaspoon baking soda
½ teaspoon baking powder
½ teaspoon salt
1½ teaspoons cinnamon
½ teaspoon ginger
1½ cups quick oats
1½ cups currants
1½ cups chopped nuts

1. Using an electric mixer, cream butter or margarine and sugar. Add molasses and eggs, blending well.

2. Combine flour, soda, baking powder, salt, cinnamon, and ginger. Add to creamed mixture, mixing thoroughly.

3. Stir in oats, currants, and nuts.

4. To make large cookies, use ¼ cup dough for each cookie. For smaller cookies, drop by heaping teaspoon. Bake on ungreased cookie sheet in pre-heated 350 degree oven for 15 minutes for the larger cookie, and 10 minutes for the smaller cookie. Cool on a wire rack.

Makes 4 dozen small cookies or 1 dozen large cookies.

Iced Sugar Cookies

We baked these heart-shaped for a wedding and decorated them with the bride and groom's names. It was a personal and unusual touch for a very special day!

½ **cup butter, softened**
1 **cup sugar**
1 **egg**
2 **tablespoons brandy**
½ **teaspoon vanilla**
2 **cups flour**
¼ **teaspoon salt**
½ **teaspoon baking powder**

1. Using an electric mixer, cream butter and sugar. Add egg, brandy, and vanilla. Beat well.

2. Combine flour, salt, and baking powder. Gradually add to creamed mixture. Mix well. Wrap and chill dough for at least 30 minutes before rolling.

3. On a lightly floured board, roll out ⅓ of the dough at a time. Roll to about ⅛" thickness and cut out with cookie cutters. Put shapes on greased baking sheets and bake in a pre-heated 400 degree oven for 10 minutes. Do not allow to brown. Cool on racks.

Icing:
1 **cup powdered sugar**
1 **egg white**
Few drops of lemon juice

1. Mix icing ingredients until smooth. Spread on cooled cookies. If desired, sprinkle with colored sugars, or pipe designs in various colors onto cookies with pastry bag.

Makes approximately 24 cookies.

Tassies

The tassie shells can be filled with various cooked and uncooked fillings such as chocolate, lemon, cream cheese, apricot preserves or fruit. The pastry is flaky and rich.

Pastry:
> **1 cup butter**
> **8 ounces cream cheese**
> **2 cups flour**
> **Dash of salt**

1. Using an electric mixer or food processor, blend butter and cream cheese. Add flour and salt, mixing well. Form dough into a ball and refrigerate until chilled, about 30 minutes to an hour.

2. Remove part of the dough, keeping the remainder in the refrigerator. Roll small amount into a ball and press into mini muffin tins that have been sprayed with vegetable coating.

3. Continue with remainder of dough, removing from refrigerator as necessary.

Filling:
> **2 eggs, lightly beaten**
> **2 teaspoons melted butter**
> **1½ cups brown sugar, packed**
> **1 cup chopped pecans or walnuts**

1. Mix eggs, butter and sugar. Add chopped nuts.

2. Fill individual uncooked pastry tarts with filling. The shells should not be too full as they will puff up during baking.

3. Bake in a pre-heated 375 degree oven for 10 to 15 minutes. Let tarts cool in pans before removing.

Note: Pastry tarts may be baked without filling for individual pastry shells. Be sure to prick each pastry shell all over before baking. Cool before removing from tins.

Makes 48 tassies.

Very Easy Sand Tarts

These are some of the first cookies my daughter, Tina, learned to make. She still includes them in her Christmas gift assortment each year. They are buttery and delicious.

1 cup butter
2 cups flour
¼ cup sugar
Pinch of salt
1 cup finely chopped pecans or walnuts
2 teaspoons vanilla
Powdered sugar

1. In large saucepan, melt butter. Add flour, sugar and salt. Mix well.
2. Stir in nuts and vanilla, blending thoroughly.
3. Form dough into small balls. Place on ungreased cookie sheet.
4. Bake in pre-heated 300 degree oven for 30 minutes or until lightly browned. Remove from oven, cool slightly, and roll in powdered sugar.

Makes 3 dozen.

Chocolate Pecan Tassies

These are scrumptious! Each one is like a bite of pecan pie, only better, because of the added chocolate chips!

1 recipe uncooked Tassie Pastry
2 large eggs
1½ cups light brown sugar
2 tablespoons butter, melted
2 teaspoons vanilla
Pinch of salt
⅔ cup semi-sweet chocolate chips
1¼ cups finely chopped pecans

1. Mix together eggs, sugar, butter, vanilla, and salt until well blended.

2. Stir in chocolate chips and pecans.

3. Fill uncooked mini pastry shells with filling. The shell should not be too full as they will puff up during baking.

4. Bake in a pre-heated 350 degree oven for 25 to 30 minutes, until the shells are a golden brown. Let the tassies cool in the pan before removing.

Makes 48 tassies.

Coconut Cluster Chocolate Drops

These are very good for Christmas gift giving! Men love them.

½ cup butter, softened
1 pound box powdered sugar
½ can sweetened condensed milk
2 teaspoons vanilla
1⅓ cups coconut
1¼ cups finely chopped pecans
2 cups semi-sweet chocolate chips
½ block Gulfwax paraffin

1. Using an electric mixer, cream butter and powdered sugar. Add sweetened condensed milk and vanilla. Blend well.

2. Stir in coconut and pecans. Refrigerate mixture until firm, about one hour.

3. Remove a small portion of the mixture at a time (keep remainder chilled). Roll about 2 teaspoons at a time into a ball. Freeze until ready to dip into chocolate.

4. Continue with remaining mixture, keeping balls in freezer until ready to dip.

Chocolate Coating:

1. In top of double boiler, melt semi-sweet chocolate chips and paraffin.

2. Removing a few candy balls from freezer at a time, quickly coat each ball with the melted chocolate mixture, using small forks or toothpicks.

3. Immediately place onto cookie sheet lined with waxed paper. Refrigerate or freeze until firm.

Makes about 72 candies.

Tart Lemon Squares

These lemon squares are so good. When we need some for a catering or a ladies tea, I use Carol Bade's wonderful recipe. I like to decorate them in the spring with a Johnny Jump-up blossom because it makes such a nice presentation.

Crust:
> 6 tablespoons butter
> ¼ cup powdered sugar
> 1 cup flour

1. In mixer or food processor, blend butter, powdered sugar, and flour. Pat mixture gently into a 9" X 9" X 2" pan. Bake in a pre-heated 350 degree oven for 20 minutes until light brown.

Filling:
> 3 eggs
> 1 cup sugar
> 3 tablespoons flour
> 4 tablespoons freshly squeezed lemon juice, strained
> Zest of ½ lemon
> Powdered sugar

1. Using an electric mixer, beat eggs lightly. Add the granulated sugar and the flour, lemon juice, and zest.
2. Pour mixture over hot crust and bake for an additional 20 minutes or until mixture appears firm. This time varies with each oven.
3. Remove from oven and sprinkle with powdered sugar while hot. Loosen custard from the edge of the pan while still warm. Cut into squares when cool.

Yields 64 1" square cookies, or 12 large squares.

Frosty Fruit Bars

Evelyn Geistweidt has been our Tea Room pastry baker for years, traveling in daily from the community of Doss, Texas. Always faithful in her commitment to her work, we have worked together on some good recipes. This is one of her recipes that is especially good during the holidays.

½ cup margarine, softened
1 cup sugar
1 egg
1 tablespoon orange zest
¼ cup pineapple or orange juice
2½ cups flour
1 teaspoon baking soda
½ teaspoon salt
½ teaspoon cinnamon
½ teaspoon nutmeg
1 cup currants
1 cup golden raisins
½ cup chopped nuts

1. Using an electric mixer, cream margarine and sugar. Add egg and mix well. Stir in orange zest and pineapple or orange juice.

2. Combine flour, soda, salt, cinnamon and nutmeg. Gradually add to creamed mixture, and blend thoroughly. Stir in currants, raisins, and chopped nuts.

3. Spread into lightly greased 11" X 17" jelly roll sheet. Bake in a pre-heated 400 degree oven for 10 to 12 minutes.

4. While warm, spread with mixture of 2 cups powdered sugar, ¼ cup milk, and ½ teaspoon vanilla.

Makes 42 large bars.

Dream Bars

A real dream of a recipe! These are fast and easy to prepare and everybody loves them. We like to serve them with our chocolate treats as a nice compliment.

½ cup butter, softened (not margarine)
1½ cups brown sugar, divided
1 cup flour
2 eggs
1½ teaspoons vanilla
½ teaspoon salt
½ teaspoon baking powder
1⅓ cups coconut
1 cup chopped pecans

1. Cream butter and ½ cup brown sugar in mixer or food processor.
2. Add flour and mix well. Press dough into ungreased 9" x 13" pan.
3. Bake in a pre-heated 350 degree oven for 10 to 15 minutes until light brown.
4. Combine remaining brown sugar, eggs, vanilla, salt and baking powder. Stir in coconut and pecans. Spread over baked layer. Bake 20 minutes more. Cool.

Makes 48 bars.

Enid's plate

Fudge Dream Bars

These are a chocoholic's dream - like a creamy slice of fudge on top of a flaky crust. Try adding a cup of coconut for a good combination.

Crust:
> 6 tablespoons butter
> 2 tablespoons sugar
> 1 cup flour
> ¼ teaspoon salt

1. Using an electric mixer or food processor, cream butter and sugar until light and fluffy.

2. Add flour and salt and mix to form a soft dough. Press dough evenly into the bottom of a 9" square pan which has been sprayed with vegetable coating.

3. Bake for 15 minutes in a pre-heated 400 degree oven until pale gold. Remove crust from oven and set aside.

4. Reduce oven temperature to 350 degrees.

Filling:
> 2 squares (2 ounces) unsweetened baking chocolate
> ¾ cup light corn syrup
> ¼ cup brown sugar
> 1 teaspoon vanilla
> ¾ cup chopped pecans
> ¼ teaspoon salt
> 2 eggs

1. In a medium saucepan, melt chocolate with light corn syrup and brown sugar over low heat. Remove from heat and stir in remaining ingredients. Pour filling onto hot crust.

2. Bake 20 to 25 minutes until puffed. Cool on wire rack.

Makes 36 squares.

Chocolate Oatmeal Brownies

Dark, rich, moist, and delicious - as good as any brownie I've ever tasted.

1 cup semi-sweet chocolate chips
⅓ cup butter or margarine
1 scant cup quick oats
¼ cup wheat germ, optional
⅓ cup non-fat dry milk powder
½ teaspoon baking powder
¼ teaspoon salt, optional
½ cup chopped walnuts or pecans
2 eggs
⅓ cup packed brown sugar
1 teaspoon vanilla

1. In the top of a double boiler or in a small heavy saucepan over very low heat, melt the chocolate chips and the butter or margarine. Remove the pan from heat, and stir the mixture until smooth. Set aside.

2. In a medium bowl combine the oats, wheat germ, dry milk powder, baking powder, salt and nuts. Set the mixture aside.

3. Using a spoon, beat the eggs in a large mixing bowl. Add the brown sugar, and the vanilla, mixing well. Stir in the melted chocolate mixture. Fold in the oats mixture until just blended. Pour the batter into a greased 8" square baking pan.

4. Bake in a pre-heated 350 degree oven for 20 to 25 minutes or until the top is crisp, but a toothpick inserted in the center of the pan comes out slightly moist. Cool completely before cutting.

Makes 25 squares.

The Peach Tree Chocolate Brownies

This is the recipe we use for our Brownie Delight served in the Tea Room. It was created when I was at market during the Tea Room's first year. The Collins cake was a flop that day and Hector, not wanting it to go to waste, came up with the idea of the ice cream and fudge sauce on top. That was a wonderful day for us - the cake was salvaged and a very popular new dessert was born!!

4 eggs
1½ cups sugar
2 teaspoons vanilla
1 cup melted butter or margarine
1½ cups Ghiradelli sweetened ground chocolate
(no substitutes)
1½ cups flour
½ teaspoon baking powder
½ teaspoon salt
1 cup chopped walnuts or pecans

1. Using a spoon, combine eggs with sugar and vanilla. Add butter or margarine.

2. Mix ground chocolate with flour, baking powder, and salt. Stir into egg mixture. Add nuts.

3. Spread into a greased 9" x 13" pan, and bake in a pre-heated 350 degree oven for 30 to 35 minutes. Cool.

Yields approximately 15 large brownies or 60 small brownies.

Layered Cheesecake Brownies

We bake these when we cater. They're an exciting addition to any dessert tray!

Brownie Base:
  1½ cups semi-sweet chocolate chips
  ¼ cup butter, room temperature
  ½ cup sugar
  2 eggs, room temperature
  1 teaspoon vanilla
  ¼ teaspoon salt
  ¼ teaspoon almond extract
  ½ cup flour

1. Spray 9" square pan with vegetable coating. Line bottom and two sides with foil that extends 2" over the side. Spray foil also.
2. Melt chocolate in microwave or in saucepan over low heat. Set aside.
3. Using an electric mixer, cream butter and beat until fluffy. Gradually add sugar and eggs, one at a time. Beat until light in color.
4. Add the vanilla, almond extract, salt, and melted chocolate.
5. Quickly add flour and mix just until blended. Pour into prepared pan. Top with Cheesecake Topping.

Cheesecake Topping:
  8 ounces cream cheese, room temperature
  2 tablespoons butter
  ½ cup sugar
  1 tablespoon flour
  2 eggs, room temperature
  2 tablespoons sour cream
  1 teaspoon vanilla

1. Using an electric mixer, beat the cream cheese and butter until fluffy.
2. Blend in sugar and flour.
3. Add eggs, sour cream and vanilla, and beat until smooth.
4. Pour mixture over uncooked brownie base. Bake in a pre-heated 350 degree oven for 45 minutes, until puffed in the center and lightly brown.

5. Cool brownies in pan for 4 hours. Cover and refrigerate for at least 2 hours. Gently lift brownies out of pan and peel off foil. Use a sharp knife dipped in hot water to cut into squares. Cover and refrigerate.

Makes 36 squares.

Tina's Peanut Butter Squares

Our daughter, Tina, who has been cooking since she was 10 years old, loves to prepare these cookies for our family. These are easy and fun to make if you need a quick dessert or a super gift for your friends!

¾ **cup brown sugar**
1 pound powdered sugar
½ **cup butter, softened**
2 cups smooth peanut butter
2 cups semi-sweet chocolate chips
1 tablespoon butter

1. Using an electric mixer, mix together first 4 ingredients thoroughly. Pat evenly into an ungreased 9" X 13" pan.
2. In saucepan melt chocolate and butter over low heat, stirring constantly. Spread over peanut mixture. Cut into bars while still warm.
3. Chill for 15 minutes and remove from pan. These keep well in the refrigerator.

Makes 48 squares.

Note: Tina bakes these in a 15" X 10" X 1" cookie sheet and cuts them (while still warm) into heart shapes.

Chocolate Revel Bars

No catering event would be complete without these. They hold up well on cookie platters, freeze beautifully, and are wonderfully delicious.

3 cups quick oats
2½ cups flour
1 teaspoon baking soda
1¼ teaspoons salt, divided
1 cup butter or margarine, softened
2 cups brown sugar, firmly packed
2 eggs
4 teaspoons vanilla, divided
1 14-ounce can sweetened condensed milk
1½ cups semi-sweet chocolate chips
2 tablespoons butter
½ cup chopped nuts

1. Combine oats, flour, soda, and 1 teaspoon salt. Set aside.

2. Using an electric mixer, beat 1 cup butter or margarine, adding brown sugar and beat until fluffy.

3. Add eggs, and 2 teaspoons vanilla to butter mixture. Beat well.

4. On low speed, add dry ingredients to beaten mixture until well combined.

5. In saucepan, heat condensed milk, chocolate chips, 2 tablespoons butter, and ¼ teaspoon salt over low heat until smooth. Remove from heat. Stir in nuts and 2 teaspoons vanilla.

6. Pat ⅔ of the oat mixture into bottom of ungreased 15" x 10" baking dish. Spread warm chocolate mixture over dough. Dot with remaining oat mixture. Press gently.

7. Bake in a pre-heated 350 degree oven for 30 to 35 minutes. Cool on a wire rack.

Makes 96 bars.

Index